1.

CW01064295

Milk glass, illuminated, NYC, 1978

Peter Blegvad

Milk

Through a Glass Darkly

Uniformbooks

First published 2023
Copyright © Peter Blegvad, and sources
ISBN 978-1-910010-36-5

Uniformbooks
7 Hillhead Terrace, Axminster, Devon EX13 5JL
uniformbooks.co.uk

Trade distribution in the UK by Central Books
centralbooks.com

Printed and bound by T J Books, Padstow, Cornwall

"que l'on s'exprime beaucoup mieux par les textes des autres."
—Chris Marker, *L'Homme et sa liberté*

"Objects always meet your obsession. Once you have an obsession, you step on it at every corner."
—Sophie Calle

Milk Bar, 1974

Q. What motivated you to start collecting quotes about milk?

A. A sense that milk harboured secrets. It had a message. Collecting quotes about it was a way to make it talk. In many voices.

Q. What about your own voice?

A. I question milk, but I can't answer for it. *Milk, Through a Glass Darkly* is a mosaic of quotes, a *cento* or literary collage. The words aren't mine, but the composition is, the order of sequence.

Q. How old were you when you began the project?

A. I was twenty. Fifty-two years ago. I'd just read about Alfred Hitchcock putting a light in a glass of milk[1] and the image seemed portentous, freighted with meaning. I began collecting quotes that confirmed my hunch that milk, even without a light in it, and despite the normalising efforts of dairies and marketing boards, is *numinous*, psychically active.

Q. You've described your 'full immersion' in milk as an initiation.

A. I knew I'd have to grow up (an initiation I dreaded) in order to decipher the message milk contained. Indeed, that *was* the message, or one of them. "I remember believing I should have to die in order to grow up, and thinking the prospect very disagreeable."—William Empson.

Q. How did you go about collecting the quotes? There was no internet when you started, fifty years ago. Did you spend a lot of time in libraries?

A. In the April 1993 issue of *Sight and Sound*, in an article entitled 'Phosphorescent Milk', I wrote "Conscious effort was not the appropriate response to what was a summons to the unconscious. I proceeded by a kind of somnambulism. With the infinite patience of idleness, I collected quotes which seemed to elucidate or compound the mystery, jotting them

1. François Truffaut, *Hitchcock/Truffaut*, in the chapter about 'Suspicion'.

down when I came across them in the course of my general reading." I confess I also looked up milk in the indexes of books and libraries and found some quotes that way, but most of the hundreds now in my files were passively amassed, acquired "serendipitously rather than by design. This guaranteed that finds were rare enough to seem oracular. It feeds obsession." That's from the section on milk I wrote for a book[2] published in 2003 to coincide with an exhibition at the British Museum devoted to Henry Wellcome's collection of medical objects. "By 1931 his collection was five times larger than the Louvre's, but for all his wealth and ambition he died before he could organise it into anything like a coherent narrative." Collecting is easy, connecting is hard.

Q. You connect groups of quotes by theme, especially at the start. Other sections seem less structured, more fluid. Is there an overall direction to the whole piece?

A. It's non-linear, rhizomatic, but I think the flow has direction, and I hope thematic resonance gives it a kind of momentum. We start with the overflowing glass, a sense of abundant potential. We end on an elegiac note, with a broken glass that "had apparently but not certainly" contained milk. En route we consider light, smell, writing, mothers, fathers, colour, nothingness, regression, gender, race, food, cattle, ectoplasm, anti-matter, the moon, sex and insanity amongst other things.

Q. Are all the quotes verbatim?

A. Barring a few minor tweaks. I was emboldened by David Shields in *Reality Hunger*: "Your uncertainty about whose words you've just read is not a bug but a feature."[3] Shields assembled his book from hundreds of quotes that go unattributed in the body of the text (though they're numbered and the authors are identified in an appendix). I've used the same approach.

---

2. 'Milk', in *The Phantom Museum*, ed. Hildi Hawkins & Danielle Olsen, Profile Books, 2003.

3. David Shields, *Reality Hunger: A Manifesto*, Knopf, 2010.

Q. Do you drink a lot of milk?

A. I don't like it. As a baby I was actually allergic to it. But what I do like are the ways milk is made strange by the imagination. Ways in which, in all ages and cultures, it has been 'saturated with providence', invested with an unstable spirit that flickers like a strobe between contraries. Milk is uncanny. It's sold to us here as pure and wholesome, but unconsciously we're aware of other milks—milks 'interior to milk'—that are anything but. I chose and organised the quotes with the aim of communicating something of that strangeness to the receptive reader.

Sources on pages 87–94

1.

Marvellously many materials make milk! Much too many to mention.

2.

You can't imagine how much milk is in a glass of milk...

3.

...the glass corresponds to the *unum vas* of alchemy and its contents to the living, semi-organic mixture from which the *lapis*, endowed with spirit and life, will emerge.

4.

Its cylindricality makes it phallic, while its hollowness makes it uterine.

5.

I put a light in the milk.
You mean a spotlight on it?
No, I put a light right inside the glass because I wanted it to be luminous.

6.

In a hollow rounded space it ended
With a luminous Lamp within suspended...

7.

What does light do specifically to milk? In a matter of minutes it destroys Vitamins A, C and B2, accelerates oxidation of fatty matter, and causes the distinctly unpleasant sensations known as "oxide taste" or "fishy taste" or "metallic flavour".

8.

What about the smell of the light?

9.

One must begin with words if one is to write. But what then of smell?

10.

... stench is the natural manifestation, in an inedible form, of femininity, of which the other natural manifestation, milk, represents the edible aspect. Vaginal odour is therefore the counterpart of the suckling function: being anterior to it, it offers an inverted image of it and can be considered to be its cause, since it precedes it in time.

11.

One need not press her too hard to draw from her at once some of that milk, more precious and fragrant than any other—smelling like the spark of flint, furtively suggesting the metallurgy of hell...

12.

(A) To make the sound μαμά... with closed lips, to mutter, moan... (B) to drink with closed lips, to suck in...

13.

To progress from word to word is to suck a nipple. Imagine saying: My dear, I am thirsty, will you let me have a little milk—This to love at first sight. But who do you think I am, says white goldenrod. Of course there is progress. Of course there are words. But I am thirsty, one might add. Yes but I love you and besides I have no milk. Oh yes, that is right. I forgot that we were speaking of words. Yet you cannot deny that to have a novel one must have milk. Not at the beginning. Granted, but at the end at least. Yes, yes, at the end. Progress from the mere form to the substance. Yes, yes, in other words: milk. Milk is the answer.

14.

It moves through the mouth like a language...

15.

I think we can safely say that when we are moved,
it is some liquid that starts moving, blood, or
milk, or salt water.

16.

...the hormone prolactin which stimulates tears
is the same hormone that produces breast milk.

17.

At their mothers' moist'ned eyes babes shall suck...

18.

Why could not water, the universal liquid, also
admit an unusual property? The water so discovered will be an invented liquid. Invention, subject
to the laws of the unconscious, suggests an
organic liquid. This could be milk.

19.

In the same way, stone and iron are produced
from water, which, however, becomes such
water as never before existed: and the earth,
too, becomes something which in itself it is not.
So also man must become that which he is not.

20.

...neither young nor old, neither modern nor
old-fashioned, neither the pupil nor the boy,
neither mature nor immature, I was neither this
nor that, I was nothing...

21.

I know what "nothing" means, and keep on playing.

22.

I had made a false entrance; I withdrew behind
a screen and began my birth over again at the
right moment, the very minute that the universe
silently called for me.

23.

When the new centre of personal energy has been
subconsciously incubated so long as to be just
ready to open into flower, "hands off" is the only
word for us, it must burst forth unaided!

24.

There's yr new life, blasted
with milk

25.

Beginning and end of the process conjoin in milk
which dissolves in weakness the old physical man
and coagulates in wisdom the new spiritual man.

26.

... and the vessel in which this spiritual birth
takes place appears as a magic vessel and as a
vessel of transformation...

27.

the iced glass is a light
it disappears tonight

28.

In what condition is this metamorphosis
completed? Not in the bright, clearly distinguish-
ing light, but in the night, which causes the
contours of things to disappear.

29.

Truth, like milk, arrives in the dark.

30.

...phosphorescent from all its encounters with darkness.

31.

Truth—the milk of the cow, if the cow itself fed on that milk.

32.

My idea was to create a general atmosphere of obscurity so as to ensure that only the object would give off light and that it would appear like a vision... I wanted to give the same effect that you get when you're in a wood and you see a butterfly.*

33.

Look upward. Neither firm nor free
Purposeless matter hovers in the dark.

34.

When the eye, coming out of darkness, suddenly sees a luminous body, it will appear much larger at first sight than after long looking at it. The illuminated object will look larger and more brilliant when seen with two eyes than with only one. A luminous object will appear smaller in size when the eye sees it through a smaller opening.

35.

...through the little hole of his wound, the immense realm of spirit enters... It has been compared with a mouth... It has a message.

---

* "It is the familiar yellow winged species that so names the Butterfly. Its German names are *Schmetterling*, from *schmetter*, meaning cream; and *Molkendieb*, meaning the Whey-thief. The association with milk in its three forms, butter, cream and whey, is remarkable."
—Frank Cowan, *Curious Facts in the History of Insects*, 1886

36.

I understood that the object contained a message for me, and I should decipher it.

37.

There
And in that state, the glass is a pool.

38.

...he discovers in the glass itself a slight deformation, which spreads deformation throughout the universe.

39.

Oh, to create my own form! To turn outward! To express myself! Let me conceive my own shape, let no one do it for me! My agitation pushes me toward writing paper.

40.

I try to approach the whiteness of the page, the pale judgement, as if I were a neophyte priest... I touch it gently, a frightened queer faced with his first female breast, a nipple that seeks attention and ministration.

41.

See, now he raises his hand
as if he wanted to give the thought
the living airy body of the word.
Eagerly dips his pen in the inkwell—
see, now he turns his face—
a deadman's eyes, large as cups,
stare darkly like one single pupil,
as he nods familiarly to the names,
thoughtfully points at his work:
and out of his bony throat he hiccups:
"You see, I'm starting to write in white!"

42.

Women, according to [Hélène] Cixous (and this is
1976), need to challenge the symbolic status quo,
and they can do so by inscribing their subjectiv-
ities, by writing what men can't: "she writes in
white ink." Mother's milk, Milky Way, white ink.

43.

What I am interested in is not the drama of being
a child but this new drama of being a mother
(yes, there are cannibals in my dreams. Yes) about
which so little has been written. Can a mother not
hold a pen? Or is it just the fact that we are all
children when we write?

44.

The act of writing, in effect, brings into play all
the libidinal impulses combined in the "polymor-
phous perversity" of infancy: the urethral libido
of flowing ink, the sado-anality of staining, the
onanistic rhythms of the hand, the pen caressing
the fecund paper "defended by its whiteness", etc.
The alphabetical characters themselves have a
libidinal charge going back to the time when the
little child was enchanted by the intrinsic configu-
rations of the letters when it began to draw.

45.

Much later, I realized that poetry writing had,
in fact, something in common with lactation.
Prompted by some mental/hormonal/godly
arrangement, the poetry comes as if from
nowhere and, if not written down, engorges a
swollen chest to the point of unbearable pain.
Eventually, the urgency begins to ease and the
writing takes place just intermittently. It is at
this point only that it can be abandoned. Then
it dries up completely. The organs which create
verse—the heart, the brain, the fingers, the
stomach—retain a memory of how it was once

done, but are no longer able to produce poetry. In fact, like lactation, poetry is something that my adopted culture—let's call it British—is not entirely sure about. While poetry writing is nothing to be ashamed of, it's certainly better done in the privacy of one's own home.

46.

… she is a helicopter and she is a bird; and there is this, the greatest wonder of all: under her tinted hair the forest murmur becomes a thought, and words issue from her breasts.

47.

This is why mothers do not write, because motherhood happens in the body as much as in the mind. I thought childbirth was a sort of journey that you could send dispatches home from, but of course it is not—it *is* home. Everywhere else is now "abroad".

48.

Every desert seems to have held a library, where the pillars of some temple lie in the sands. The traveller may still see the site of the bookroom of Rameses that was called the *Hospital of the Soul.* There was a library at the breast of the Sphinx…

49.

One learns at the breast; what does one learn at the breast? What can we be taught by milk?

50.

Whom shall he teach knowledge? and whom shall he make to understand doctrine? Them that are weaned from the milk and drawn from the breast.

51.

For everyone that useth milk is unskilful in the word of righteousness: for he is a babe.

52.

The breast-feeding fatwa came in mid-May. A religious scholar wrote that there had been instances in the time of the prophet when adult women breast-fed adult men in order to avoid the need for women to wear a veil in front of them.

"A woman at work can take off the veil or reveal her hair in front of someone she has breast-fed", wrote the scholar Izat Atiyah.

The ruling was mocked on satellite television shows, and was quickly condemned. Mr. Atiyah was suspended from his job, ridiculed in newspapers and within days issued a retraction, saying it was a "bad interpretation of a particular case".

53.

When I was a baby I drank milk, and now I smoke tobacco.
You're a free person. Do as you please.
I may, but you may not.
Why is that so?
Because I'm a man and you're a woman.
What is all right for a man is not always all right for a woman.

54.

Then the three ice-shapes stooped down and sat with their knees drawn up and let the sun melt them. As milk they melted, and the milk ran into the mouths of the sleepers, and the sleepers woke.

55.

The sleep was no chance sleep; it was the sleep of initiation.

56.

Insomnia drank a milk of light, poison more certain than hemlock milk. And yet the same drink was a philtre for loves which believed themselves eternal and peaceful, under the trees, in the depths of parks.

57.

According to an Indian version of Cinderella, the heroine is seventh of seven daughters, all of whom wed the Prince. Cinderella, having unjustly fallen under a cloud of suspicion, the children say to their father: "Let your seventh wife who is in the dungeon come forth. Place seven curtains between her and us and see what happens." Cinderella is brought forth and seven curtains are placed between her and the children. Three streams of milk spring from her breasts and, penetrating the seven curtains, run into the children's mouths.

58.

The situation is much the same with the bosom room here. Milk gushes out from the crack under the locked door, and a white, sickly sweet smell wafts through the keyhole and turns my stomach. Not a sound issues from the room, it is governed by the silence of the lying-in bed. I know this deep soft silence all too well from past times. In those days I had wanted it to last for ever. But now?... Everything has become terribly different, and so the bosom room simply fills me with despair.

59.

I only now noticed thin trickles of a white milky fluid moving among the debris, collecting in pools here and there. These white pools continually widened as the liquid eroded their edges, eating away whatever came in contact with it; it was only a question of time before the entire mass of wreckage would be disposed of in this way. I stood still for a moment to watch the process, fascinated by such a practical, thorough method of clearance.

60.

...is not our own interior white on the chart?

61.

In 1938 the Viennese analyst Otto Isakower
published his classic paper entitled 'A Contribution to the Patho-Psychology of Phenomena
Associated with Falling Asleep' describing what
has come to be termed "the Isakower phenomenon". As described by a later researcher, this
hypnagogic event is characteristically remem-
bered or re-experienced by the individual as the
visual sensation of a large, doughy, shadowy
mass, usually round, growing larger as it comes
nearer and nearer to his face, swelling to a gigantic size and threatening to crush him, and then
gradually growing smaller and moving further
away. Often there is an indistinct perception of a
purplish shape like the nipple area of the breast.
The approaching mass slowly seems to become
a part of him, obscuring the boundaries between
his body and the outside world, and blurring his
sense of self more and more.

62.

Everything was expanding in blackness. Inflating
and widening, yet at the same time shrinking and
straining, evading something, and some kind of
winnowing, general and particular, a coagulating
tension and a tensing coagulation, a dangling by a
fine thread, as well as transformation into something, transmutation, and furthermore—a falling
into some cumulative, towering system, and as
if on a narrow little plank raised six stories up,
together with the excitement of all organs. And
tickling.

63.

The supreme boon desired for the Indestructible
Body is uninterrupted residence in the Paradise

of the Milk that Never Fails: "Rejoice ye with
Jerusalem, and be glad with her, all ye that love
her: rejoice for joy with her, all ye that mourn
for her: that ye may suck, and be satisfied with
the breasts of her consolations; that ye may milk
out, and be delighted with the abundance of her
glory."

64.

...Over the silver mountaines,
Where spring the Nectar fountains.
And there Ile kisse
The bowle of blisse,
And drinke my eternall fill
On every milken hill.

65.

The picture given of the heart is that from being
comparatively cold, hard, small, low and dry, it
becomes progressively warmer, softer, larger,
higher, and finally releases a flow of liquid.
Almost the complete picture is given in the
following passage from St. Bernard:
"Often we... begin to pray with a heart luke-
warm and dry. But if we steadily persist, grace
comes steadily in a flood upon us, our breast
grows full of increase, a wave of piety fills our
inward heart; and if we press on, the milk of
sweetness conceived in us will spread over us
in fruitful flood."

66.

Soul and body food, heart's ease, is the gift of
'All Heal', the nipple inexhaustible.

67.

Its opacity and unwonted consistency made an
unknown substance of it, a substance charged
with phosphorescences...

68.

...like digging at the base of a tree in the back-
yard and finding no roots at all but, instead, a
bed of uranium, a strange substance...

69.

...the object... only becomes real when desire
permits it to be other than it is.

70.

The real will from its crude compoundings come,
Seeming, at first, a beast disgorged, unlike,
Warmed by a desperate milk.

71.

I have a horror of milk. It never smoothed my
way into the world, I sucked my Father's gum of
ground pearls and saline...

72.

...my face a rash of rage my neck stiff with blood
ropes spithowlcurse o god o god o god o god a
gulp of milk splashed my nose pinched but I will
not swallow strangling speech curdling the milk o
god o god o god gurgling flying in a mist of milk o
god o god soaked with milk dribbling spittle o god

73.

...it is difficult to localize the artist's rage, which,
like the milk, overflows, so that there is no telling
where it may go. At first the anger seems directed
at the glass, but it might just as well be aimed at
the milk, which opens up a myriad of symbolic
possibilities.

74.

Wring the neck of all sick inventions born in that
progressive white wake.

75.

I want the old rage, the lash of primordial milk.

Look, look, the ditch is running white!
I've more veins than a tree!

76.

Oh! What great tree of light
found here the source of its milk? We
have not fed on that milk!

77.

And in that loss a self-effacing tree,
Color of context, imperceptibly
Rustling with its angel, thus turns the waste
To shade and fiber, milk and memory.

78.

Then the leaves of the tree commenced to rustle
and a fine milk-white rain dripped from them
upon the White Youth. A warm zephyr was felt,
the tree creaked, and from under its roots a female
being arose up to her waist… The goddess offered
the Youth milk from her swelling breasts, and
having drunk, he felt how his powers had grown
a hundred-fold.

79.

There is a part of me, I have realized, that wants to
nurse the stranger on the bus. Or perhaps it wants
to nurse the bus itself, or the tree I see through the
window of the bus, or the child I once was, paying
my fare on the way home from school.

80.

[Bertram] Lewin's "dream screen" constitutes the
background on which the dream projects its imag-
ing: it is flat, or virtually so, like the surface of the
earth, for it is genetically a segment of the baby's
vast picture of the mammary hemisphere.

81.

A monstrous little potbelly
considering the surface of reality with the
gaze of its flabbergasted belly button.

82.

What whiteness will you add to this whiteness,
what candor?

83.

...the white of a clarity beyond the facts

84.

On the bottle standing in front of him the white
label bearing the words "White Label" made
perfectly clear what intense degree of whiteness the contents of this receptacle would have
allowed one to attain, a whiteness composed
negatively of a whole annihilated world, and positively of the floral patterns of hoar-frost settling
on the walls of the vitrified brain like frail bones
which would perhaps later be covered with new
flesh.

85.

...the most simple of subjects: an American bar.
The clientele drink whiskey; a policeman's arrival
is announced; the whiskey is hidden and replaced
with milk; the policeman enters; the clients decap-
itate him, seat his corpse on a chair and perform
tragic dances around his head.

86.

The policeman grows fatter each day and rivals
the new tanks. He blots out the doorway of the
little café. A couple seeing him spills the milk at
the counter, remembering what they did under
the bridge last night.

87.

…here, there's no language
for *officer* or *law*, no color to call *white*.
if snow fell, it'd fall black…

88.

Indeed, what credit would snow deserve for
being white if its matter were not black, if it did
not come from the depths of its hidden being to
crystallize into whiteness?

89.

That is, hot ice and wondrous strange snow.
How shall we find the concord of this discord?

90.

White… has a peculiar twofold quality. On the
one hand, it is the supreme fulfillment, the
integration of all the richness to which particular
colours can add up. But on the other hand, it is
also the absence of hue and therefore of life. It
has the purity of the innocent, who have not yet
lived, and the emptiness of the dead, for whom
life is over.

91.

Duality must exist for the imagination to be
engaged: there must be a "dual participation of
desire and fear, a participation of good and evil,
a peaceful participation of black and white" for
the material element to involve the entire soul.

92.

…the dream excels at uniting contraries and in
representing them in a single object.

93.

…an object that you can interrogate   …this
object will be packed   it will be something like
a condenser   filled with energy   organized

energy   that came from someplace and can go
some other place

94.

…when it appears independent of any general
notion and detached from the sanity of a cause,
isolated and inexplicable in the light of ignorance,
then and then only may it be a source of enchantment.

95.

And there is no object so soft but it makes a hub
for the wheeled universe.

96.

All this, through the writing. He closes his eyes
and sees thick blobs of text on paper. Pen rolls
out of hand. From across the galaxy, the room,
the object stares at him and sighs.

97.

It is like a glass of milk. We need the glass. And
we need the milk.

98.

milk is subtle, supple, shifting, ever ready to
become something other than itself.

99.

The ambiguity of milk is heightened when
erotic overtones are attributed to this maternal
substance, when emotions more appropriate to
the genital site are carried to the breast. This
happens quite often, of course, for Indian eroticism has always placed enormous emphasis
upon breasts swelling like mangoes.

100.

…I collect black and white. From the standpoint
of white all color is color. From the standpoint of

black. Black is white. White is black. Black is black. White is black. White and black is black and white.

101.

I eat only white foods: eggs, sugar, shredded bones, the fat of dead animals, rice, turnips, sausages in camphor, pastry, cheese (the white varieties), cotton salad, and certain kinds of fish (skinned).

102.

Custom reconciles us to everything. If our mothers had fed us human flesh from infancy, who amongst us would reject it in later years?

103.

As with most mammals, our first taste of sweetness comes with our mother's milk. It could be that we acquire a taste for it at the breast, or we may be born with an instinct for sweet things that makes us desire mother's milk.

104.

Even in the case of so-called clean meat, like beef, the same people who eat the muscle flesh of cattle are revolted at the thought of eating their eyes, their brains, their testicles, their lungs. They would vomit if they had to drink blood. Why? The question is pointless: distaste for certain body parts, and particularly for body fluids in their fluid state, belongs to the penumbra of taboo, well outside the realm of rational explanation.

105.

I review all the flavours I have tasted in my life to try to recognise this multiple flavour, and I arrive at an opposite but perhaps equivalent sensation which is that of the milk for an infant, since as the first flavour it contains all flavours.

106.

…you can hardly tell where one flavour ends and
the next begins. That's Mother's Milk by Suicide
Bunny. The name isn't an accident…

107.

White foods taste best to me

and I prefer to eat alone. I don't know why.
Once I heard girls singing a May Day song that went:

> Violante in the pantry
> Gnawing at a mutton bone
> How she gnawed it
> How she clawed it
> When she felt herself alone.

[…]

But by now the day is wide open and a strange
                              young April light
is filling the moor with gold milk.

108.

Although milk seems to be white in color, due to
the reflection and dispersion of light in the fat
globules and other solids, actually it is faintly
yellow… Certain American paper money is
printed in yellow because of this basic hue of
milk…

109.

Men think that there is such a thing as white,
black, sweet or bitter; but in truth the universe
is composed of "thing" and "nothing".

110.

There was no word or term which could further
report the vision of nothing on the other side.
Nothing was all; there was no other word for it
but "white".

111.

What horror to awake at night
and in the dimness see the light.
   Time is white
   mosquitoes bite
I've spent my life on nothing.

112.

In the white endlessness
How pure and big a wound
His imagination left.

113.

no whiteness (lost) is so white as the memory of
whiteness.

114.

I lost the body of a child, a child's body, the eyes
of a child... and I was afraid, and I went back to
find it... and I can't find it!

115.

What is this death but a whitening, a carrying of
whiteness to ultra-white...

116.

Absolute white. White whiter than all whiteness... White, mad, exasperated, shrieking with
whiteness. Fanatical, furious, riddling the eyeball.

117.

Memory of all other colors fell away and he lolled
in the inarticulate shine. There was no explanation and it illuminated nothing.

118.

It was this white garment of mourning which he
still wore, the white mourning of surgical gowns
so much more significant than black, since white
is the colour of obliteration whereas black, far

from being the colour of emptiness and nothingness, is much more the active shade which
makes the deep and therefore dark substance of
all things… black as congealed blood or charred
wood, but much less lugubrious than the deathly
restfulness of white. Yet this desert whiteness did
not rule out all subsequent possibilities, when
it too would coagulate to form directions in the
blood and when it too would know the three
congruences of putrefaction.

119.

…it is hard to say whether the object of desire is
the incandescence of life or of death. The incandescence of life means death; death means an
incandescence of life.

120.

Defunct Reason was prowling around him like
a phantom and accompanied him to the abyss,
which it illuminated with a sepulchral glimmer.
…this is what he called "the headlight for drown-
ing himself".

121.

…Any little one will kill himself for milk.

122.

…if I have yet to join the hosts of the suicides,
it is because (fatigue apart) I find it no meaning-
fuller to drown myself than to go on swimming.

123.

The sea is a room far back in time
Lit by the headlights of a passing car
A glass of milk glows on the table
Only you can reach it for me now.

124.

The glass of milk stands as a symbolic plenum

sacrificed to a hand that simply cannot reach out to grasp it. The absence of any obvious obstacle to gratification suggests an internal constraint—an inhibition rather than a prohibition.

125.

My mother told me that she became pregnant while still nursing me. Slowly I realized that this other child, my brother, had absorbed all the nourishment away from me, thus leaving me without marrow in my bones.

126.

Beneath the teats she drew the outline of a small child reaching for the breast. While making it, she commented, "There's only room here for one baby. There's no room for a second baby. I meant to have Romulus and Remus." As she said this she smiled, recognizing that she had expressed her unconscious impulse to keep her own baby brother away from the mother. "No competition here", she said.

127.

I am very hungry when I drink.
    I need to leave it when I have it held,
    They will be white with which they know they see, that darker makes it be a color white for me, white is not shown when I am dark indeed with red despair...

128.

Water is also white, the harmony, the purity, the innocence, the source of everything on earth.

129.

White water which is pure is as inconceivable as clear milk.

130.

On the sixteenth day you will find the plate
dissolved into a white water like milk. Change the
dung every fourth day, complete this water, and
this is the philosophic oil, a water penetrating
and quieting, lighting candles and illuminating
the house, and whereby all philosophers are
sustained.

131.

My sister is the beautiful day. Oh beautiful day,
my sister, wipe my nose, swaddle me in fresh-
smelling garments. I nurse at the adamantine
nipple of the beautiful day. I quaff the milk of the
beautiful day, and for the first time since 1956,
I cheese on the shoulder of the beautiful day.

132.

Cheese is philosophically interesting as a food
whose qualities depend on the action of bacteria
—it is, as James Joyce remarked, "the corpse of milk".

133.

Cheese: milk's great leap for immortality.

134.

The light of cheese is undoubtedly bacterial or
fungal in origin, but information on the organism
responsible is lacking, and no recent cases of luminous cheese appear to have been recorded.

135.

The art historian Pamela Simpson notes that
butter sculpture was a medium "strongly
associated with women". While making butter for
home use, women had long used molds to mark
their product, and the shaping of butter was born
of rural homemaking. The journey from butter-
making to butter sculpting was, apparently, a
natural route. And butter sculpture wasn't exactly

unusual: one historian notes that butter statuary was so popular that, by 1876, it was a common feature on the exhibition circuit.

136.

And the beavers building Babel
Beneath each tree's thin beard,
Said, "Is it Cain and Abel
Fighting again we heard?"
It is Ass-Face, Ass-Face,
Drunk on the milk of the stars...

137.

Asses' milk... resembles human milk more closely than almost any other milk from animals, with the exception of the fat, which is low in asses' milk.

138.

Why is the milk of brown women better than that of white?
Because brown women are hotter than others, and heat purges the milk, and so it is better.
Why have not birds and fish milk and paps?
Because paps would hinder the flight of birds: the fish also have neither paps nor milk, as Aristotle saith, but the females cast much spawn, on which the male touches with a small gut, which causes their kind to be infinite in succession.

139.

Once I was ordinary—
Sat by my father's bean tree
Eating the fingers of wisdom.
The birds made milk
When it thundered I hid under a flat stone.

140.

...thunder is the natural enemy of milk, which it tends to curdle and destroy.

141.

Thunder is a vibration of the air that cannot
affect milk in any way. What does cause milk to
turn sour during stormy weather, however, is the
formation of bacteria that convert the sugar in
milk into lactic acid.

142.

...milk and storms fade more or less together

143.

Time's tune my ladies with the teats of music,
The scaled sea-sawers, fix in naked sponge
Who sucks the bell-voiced Adam out of magic,
Time, milk and magic, from the world beginning...

144.

You see this one-eyed midget
shouting the word "Now!"
You say "For what reason?"
and he says "How?"
You say "What does this mean?"
and he screams back "You're a cow!
Give me some milk or else go home!"

145.

I got a good milk cow
but her head is hard like a block of wood.
She's a number one Jersey cow
but her head is hard like a block of wood.
Boys, it's a mighty tough titty
but the milk is so doggone good.

146.

Angels of cotton-wool,
Indecent and dirty,
On the grass milk the udders of big
Geographical cows.

147.

We milk the cow of the world, and as we do
We whisper in her ear, "You are not true".

148.

"Milk the cow, burned child, and bring back all
the milk," said the stepmother, who used to rake
the ashes and milk the cow, once upon a time,
but the burned child did all that, now. The ghost
of the mother went into the cow. "Drink milk,
grow fat," said the mother's ghost. The burned
child pulled on the udder and drank enough milk
before she took the bucket back and nobody saw,
and time passed, she drank milk every day, she
grew fat, she grew breasts, she grew up. There
was a man the stepmother wanted and she
asked him into the kitchen to get his dinner, but
she made the burned child cook it, although the
stepmother did all the cooking before. After the
burned child cooked the dinner the stepmother
sent her off to milk the cow. "I want that man
for myself," said the burned child to the cow. The
cow let down more milk, and more, and more,
enough for the girl to have a drink and wash her
face and wash her hands. When she washed her
face, she washed the scabs off and now she was
not burned at all, but the cow was empty. "Give
your own milk, next time," said the ghost of the
mother inside the cow. "You"ve milked me dry."

149.

A farmer had milked his cow to death. It all began
when his wife said, Go milk Bossy.
　　No, no, no! It's not that way with us anymore.
　　Go milk Bossy or she'll burst. Then the bull'll
lose his mind, said his wife.
　　No, no, no! I've fallen in love with a turkey hen.
　　You better milk Bossy or she'll burst. Then the
bull'll lose his mind and we'll have a mental case
in the barn, said his wife.

No, no, no! I want to take the turkey hen up
to the bedroom and play with her feet, I want to
open the bed and put her on her back and crawl
between her drumsticks.

But first milk Bossy before she explodes and the
bull loses his mind, said his wife.

When the farmer finally got to the barn, Bossy
had swollen into a huge milk bag standing on its
four dugs. The bull, watching at the window, his
hooves covering his ears.

The farmer began to milk Bossy. When the
milk turned pink he said, Oh, how dainty. When
the milk turned red he said, Why not? Where is it
written that milk has always to be white?

Finally only a parched piece of cowhide...

It was then the bull lost his mind, and was
last seen in the distance as something rather tiny
stampeding in a pasture the size of a postage
stamp...

150.

[The cow] ...has cream caramel on its udders. So
all the people, judges, kings and queens, and all
the bishops come to lick its udders. It even licks
its own. A bad trouble because the caramel comes
from its belly button. It's dripping all over him...
And the cow drank up its own burnt udders.

151.

The quarrel between the boiled chicken and the
                                                            ventriloquist
had for us the meaning of a cloud of dust
which passed above the city
like the blowing of a trumpet
[...]
It blew so loudly
that its nose cracked open like a nut
and the nut spat out
into the far distance
a little cow-shed

wherein the youngest calf
was selling its mother's milk
in sausage-skin flasks
that its father had vulcanised.

152.

... outside the cities even replete with the
boiled milk the dealer brings us redolent of thyme
(lavender) the circulatory system regurgitates
the myrtle in the stomach (ovary) of the
ruminant: and we summon the cow of pleasure
to the border of that land slowly with its rope
(not knowing why or where) the seat of the Mother
a stump to sit herself on, great Obstetrician: and
the Obstinate one turns to call us where the
flowing milk sprinkles our clothes:
a breeding horse mounts the cow, father:
and at its feet the old man collects the milk
at dawn his shadow (falling): a herd of sows
and the grazing seal of two feet stamp
nine steps: porcelain ripped from the white
clay the first commercial sounds, breakfast.

153.

According to a *New York Times* article in August
1997, the student handbook of the Citadel requires
first-year cadets to memorise standard, quirky
responses to traditional questions posed during
shakedowns by upper-classmen. For instance,
the answer to the question, how much milk
is left in the carton (which is expressed by the
upper-classmen as "How is the cow?") must be
answered, "Sir, she walks, she talks, she's full of
chalk, the lacteal fluid extracted from the female
of the bovine species is highly prolific to the X
degree, sir! (with X representing the number of
glassfuls left)" Any other answer by a cadet would
be punishable.

154.

The cow is of the bovine ilk;
One end is moo, the other milk.

155.

In Uganda men become warmly attached to their
cows; some of them they love like children, pet
and talk to them, and weep over their ailments.
Should a favorite cow die, their grief is extreme
and cases are not wanting in which men have
committed suicide through excessive grief at the
loss of an animal.

156.

As you also know, his death was as self-denying
as his life, for he died through his faith in a
hygienic mixture of chalk and water as a substi-
tute for milk, which beverage he regarded as
barbaric, and as involving cruelty to the cow.

157.

My mind misgives me at the memory of many
merciless men, who may monthly be marked
in our mighty metropolis, like morbid, morbid
monsters, mauling and mercilessly misusing
the mild milch cows! Murky misanthropes!
Much do they merit manacles!

158.

Frank Leslie's Illustrated Weekly of May 8, 1858,
documents the deplorable sanitary conditions
in the Husted and Wilson distilleries at Skillman
Street and Franklin Avenue in Brooklyn. A writer
and staff artist were repeatedly attacked in their
attempts to record the details of this operation:
the 1,200 cramped and filthy stalls rented to the
various milkmen, the diseased and dying animals,
the careless handling of manure, and the water-
ing of milk. The cows chained in these dark and
unsanitary conditions would be fed on grain

mash, or slop, a waste product of the distillery process. The thin blue milk given by these cows was doctored with chemical whiteners to give it the appearance of healthy milk.

In the aftermath of a fire, a complex of unsanitary underground milch-cow stables was discovered on the Lower East Side of Manhattan. The badly burned and ulcerated cows, fed on the by-products of local distilleries, were still being milked for commercial purposes. The owners were fined.

159.

There was a great fear of modern speed. Early railway travellers were anxious of the effects that those new velocities might have on their bodies, and it was speculated that cows in fields nearby a passing train would have their milk turned black.

160.

Udder Table depicts society's dependency on milk while also celebrating the cow and her teats. Milk makes the human strong and healthy, thus dairy has become emblematic of America. However, the cow seems to be appreciated only when doused in ketchup and slapped between buns. This totemic table is a reminder to an overly sanitized society that milk comes from a teat, not a refrigerated carton at the supermarket. *Udder Table* glorifies the bovine mammary gland and bestows the cow with the totemic status she deserves for the production of America's favorite beverage.

161.

The whole udder filled
The udder must be available in one or two complete pieces. When it is cooked to soft and skinned, cut it lengthwise with several trenches but not to the ground. Then prepare good, very fine minced meat, mix it with a few egg yolks.

This is filled between each trench. The udder
is squeezed back into shape. A measure of sour
cream, mixed with a few egg yolks, is spread over
the udder. Bestrew it with bread crumbs and bake
it a little in the oven until it gets a nice colour. It
is served with sauce.

162.

For an udder to be eaten, some rabbis felt it must
be cut open and its milk removed by cutting it
in its length and breadth and then pressing it
against a well. Others maintain that it's not neces-
sary, as only that milk which has passed through
the udder of a live animal qualifies as milk under
the meat/milk prohibition. The milk found in the
udder of a slaughtered cow is not milk under this
law. Similarly, an infant is permitted to drink its
mother's milk via a nipple of flesh, as the milk in
the breast is not yet considered milk, but pareve.*

163.

At church
If you fellate a gentleman before receiving
communion, be careful not to swallow his cum.
Otherwise you will have broken your fast, which
is strictly against religious practice. [Except on
Fridays: sperm, like milk, is not classified by the
church as a meat product.]

164.

...the cream separator has cut a cow in half,
and the automatic milker jack boys off to white
bone juice...

165.

The Logos is not only milk but also semen...

---

* Denoting or relating to a foodstuff made without milk, meat,
or their derivatives, and therefore permissible to be eaten with
both meat and dairy dishes according to Jewish dietary laws.

According to ancient physiology, the female could turn blood into milk and the male could turn it into semen. Blood, milk and semen were variations of the same essential substance.

166.

The peculiar visual correspondence between milk and semen as vital sexual fluids—both white and apportioned respectively between women and men—accorded perfectly with the traditional Western notion of nature as a balance of binary opposites.

167.

Taking the size of the body into account, man emits more sperm than any other animal. [...] It is white in all cases, and Herodotus is wrong when he says that the Aethiopians eject black sperm.

168.

The boy, identified as "Billy", peers out from behind an oversized glass of milk, his expression both slyly submissive and boldly defiant. With a milk moustache that imitates Adolf Hitler's, he promotes the cocktail bluntly called "Nazi Milk". [...] The overdetermined shape of Billy's moustache suggests the well-worn psychological notion that, if virtue is a product of repression, it will be manifested politically as a youth-fixated, authoritarian paternalism and sexually as latent homosexuality. By invoking fellatio, the picture implied a perverse transubstantiation of the milk into semen as it touched the boy's lips.

169.

On another occasion, when Cabaner was out, Rimbaud found his daily glass of milk and neatly ejaculated into it.

170.

Not painful but certainly odd was his request one
afternoon that we should both masturbate on to
a plate and then, on our hands and knees, lap it
up like pussy cats. I went through with this but
found, and still find, it a rather melancholy and
depressing moment in my erotic life probably
because it was, of necessity, post-orgasmic. Not so
ELT and in later years, long after we'd abandoned
any sexual contact, he would mention it to me
with a kind of retrospective glee.

171.

An odd, violent milk
Teems in the bowels of the firmament;
A snail climbs and disturbs
The serenity of the clouds.

172.

The moon sailed from behind the clouds, yet it
was not the moon, it was the pupa. A pupa of
tremendous size atop the trees. A child's pupa
atop the world.

173.

...the soul of the man who is to be reborn goes
to the moon, pours down onto the earth as rain...
goes into plants... is eaten (by a man) and trans-
forms into semen that impregnates a woman.

174.

Now, you will ask me what in the world we
went up on the Moon for; I'll explain it to you.
We went to collect the milk, with a big spoon
and a bucket. Moon-milk was very thick, like a
kind of cream cheese. It formed in the crevices
between one scale and the next, through the
fermentation of various bodies and substances
of terrestrial origin which had flown up from
the prairies and forests and lakes, as the Moon

sailed over them. It was composed chiefly of vegetal juices, tadpoles, bitumen, lentils, honey, starch, crystals, sturgeon eggs, moulds, pollens, gelatinous matter, worms, resins, pepper, mineral salts, combustion residue. You had only to dip the spoon under the scales that covered the Moon's scabby terrain, and you brought it out filled with that precious muck.

175.

… for some, the moon is the breast and the eye of night.

176.

Castratos of moon-mash

177.

I drank till I sank in a swoon
and dreamt I sucked gin from a nipple in the moon.

178.

Moondrop: a liquid of magical potency, supposed to be shed by the moon.

179.

And spermatozoa
At the core of Nothing
in the milk of the Moon

180.

Like a milkmaid
In twilight
Your fingertips tug
The secret sources of light
Till you—pierced by the
Trial of evening—
Deliver your eyes
To the Moon, for the nightwatch.

181.

...it was time for rough magic: to cast the spell
I had to place each blue object (two marbles, a
miniature feather, a shard of azure glass, a string
of lapis) into my mouth, then hold them there
while they discharged an unbearable milk.

182.

l'heure bleue, hour of doorsteps lit by milk

183.

As James Joyce's vision failed he took to wearing
a milkman's uniform while writing. Supposedly
he believed it caught the sunlight and reflected it
down on his page.

184.

...I was poulticing my thirst with apples, slaking care,
When suddenly I felt a whir of dread. Soon, soon,
Stiff as a bone, I listened for the Milkman's tread.
I heard him softly bang the door of the huge truck
And then his boots besieged my private yard. I tried
To keep my eyes speared to the table, but the suck
Of apprehension milked my force. At last he mounted
My backstairs, climbed to the top, and there he stood still
Outside the bolted door. The sun's colour fainted.
I felt the horror of his quiet melt me, steal
Into my sockets, and seduce me to him from
My dinner. His hand clung round the latch like rubber.
I felt him ooze against the screen and shake the frame.
I had to slide the bolt; and thus I was the robber
Of my porch. Breathing smiling shape of fright,
The Milkman made his entrance; insistent donor,
He held in soft bleached hands the bottled sterile fruit,
And gave me this fatal, this apostate dinner.

185.

here is where the notion of "form" begins to
break down   what about form?   form is a notion

arrived at by subtraction   a residue   in the sense
that the form of the milk is its bottle

186.

I see the rays approaching, the poison of corpses
to be unloaded on my body, the rotten cadavers
of friends entombed in milk bottles...

187.

One newspaper article described how parents
were being supplanted by eerie doppelgangers.
Only children could spot the subtle differences.
For a time, affected children found a gritty
substance in their school milk. At first poison
was suspected but it turned out to be sand from
a beach hundreds of miles away. Despite police
investigations none of the impostors were ever
positively identified and there was a growing
belief in the community that they might not
even be human. The impostors vanished as inex-
plicably as they had arrived when the children's
real, bewildered parents were found wandering
on the very same beach from which the sand
had originated. They had no idea how they had
arrived there, how long they had been away or
what had happened during their absence.

188.

At midnight, Dr. Polidori recorded in his diary,
as Mary nursed her four-month-old baby, the
group "really began to talk ghostly. L[ord] B[yron]
repeated some verses of Coleridge's 'Christabel',
of the witch's breast; when silence ensued,
and Shelley, suddenly shrieking and putting his
hands to his head, ran out of the room with a
candle. Threw water in his face and gave him
ether. He was looking at Mrs. S[helley], and
suddenly thought of a woman he had heard of
who had eyes instead of nipples, which, taking
hold of his mind, horrified him."

189.

"Well, a child is a child," I thought to myself, and I imagined labor, wet nurses, illnesses, exudative skin rashes, child-related messiness and living expenses, and I thought that an infant, with its milk and baby warmth, would destroy the girl, turning her into a lubberly, warm little mommy.

190.

... Frida appears to be simultaneously protected by the nurse and offered as a sacrificial victim.

Nor does Frida look like a sleepy, satisfied, cuddled infant. The piercing look she gives the viewer seems to say that along with the milk, which she described as "saturated with providence", she also imbibes a terrible knowledge of her own fate.

191.

The scattering of light rays within milk gives it an appearance both dense and luminous. Milk's unique receptivity to light causes it to shine forth as if internally illuminated, as if brightness itself were made fluid. Milk thus shares in the allure possessed by all glowing things.

192.

It has been said that true albinos produce light of a similar luminescence when they move their bowels.

193.

Her milk is my shit

194.

It is a well-known fact that no one ever sees the sun in a dream, although one is often aware of some far brighter light. Material objects and human bodies are illumined through their own agencies.

195.

… each substance in its chemical composition is endowed with a 'phosphorescence'(?) and lights up like luminous advertisements not quite.

196.

So much inner light suggests matter's intelligence.

197.

Is not every form of light a speck of fire, a glowing body? Are we not ourselves a glowing spark of life? The light temperature of the eye is the measure of this glowing, consciousness is its character. And thus everything which we regard as finite must be in a state of glowing.

198.

And, there and then, there rose up that motif, in itself banal but which was about to modulate into infinite variations: milk cures poison. The ancient formula shone out in an explosion of white light. He was swimming bedazzled in a milky radiance, irradiated by stars of lily-white matter and marguerites, while the poisons of all the plants circulated in his veins. But he was drinking in a celestial life at a breast from which there flowed a miraculous milk of stars and snow-crystals. No longer only one woman's breast that a mouth has bitten to diffuse the voluptuous juice, as the broken euphoria generously delivers up its sap, the torn celandine its orange-coloured liquid to which the butterflies come to bathe and embellish their wings; a gap was opening in the clouds from which, in a cataract, there streamed down the non-existent whiteness, and he was passing through the torments of death and the delirium of resurrections.

199.

Os′te·o·pho′to·car′di·ol′o·gy
Bones, lights and hearts. Bones to begin with.
Light in the form of scintillation, illuminating,
lighting up. One of the most brilliant words,
because of "photo". Like superillumination.

200.

Madness was finding oneself permanently in
an all-embracing unreality. I called it the "Land
of Light" because of the brilliant illumination,
dazzling, astral, cold, and the state of extreme
tension in which everything was...

201.

at the bottom of the most utterly
   forgotten nightmares
an airtight cell, out of which
primal light flashes

(the full force of it, flooding a living
man, even if blind and draped in black,
   would kill)

202.

I remember believing I should have to die in order
to grow up, and thinking the prospect very disagreeable.

203.

The idea of this rebirthing ritual was that Candace
would form a loving, affectionate bond with her
adoptive mother.
   But just ten minutes into the procedure, the
little girl complained that she was tired, she
couldn't breathe, couldn't push her way out.
Eleven minutes and 35 seconds into the session
she cried: "I'm gonna die. Please, please, I can't
breathe." After 21 minutes, she wept: "I'm throwing up".

However, Watkins and her assistants kept pressing in on her, taunting her as a "quitter" and a "twerp".

"You want to die? OK, then, die," said one assistant. "You got to push hard if you want to be born," jeered another.

By the time an hour had elapsed, Candace had said she was dying 11 times and the only sound emanating from her petrified form was a faint whimpering.

Ten minutes later, Jeane Newmaker asked her daughter: "Baby, do you want to be born?"

From the motionless bundle in the middle of the room came a barely audible: "No." It was the last word Candace Newmaker uttered.

204.

The grail broken,
the light gone from the glass,
we would make it
anew.

205.

When childhood dies, its corpses are called adults
and they enter society, one of the politer names
of hell. That is why we dread children, even if we
love them; they show us the state of our decay.

206.

A dead person's fatless shade
Whirls in black oblivion shivering
For the icy slitherings of ghosts is all there is out there
When suddenly it finds itself
Drawn to a distant glimmer then
Looking into an enchanted cave
A light-filled paradise of warm jewels
A little kingdom of splendor and beatitudes
In the region known as essence of desire
Which though never sated is forever satisfied.

Lured by the exhilarating smell
The shade
Enters
And sleeps
Only to awake riveted
Rooted in a uterus
A ghastly fetus doomed to one more round
Of procreative desperation...

207.

Cell by cell the baby made herself, the cells
Made cells. That is to say
The baby is made largely of milk.

208.

...he who will not work... gives birth to wind,
but he who is willing to work gives birth to his
own father.

209.

...she thought—it was blasphemous—...that the
Christ was somehow father to himself, had ferti-
lized the egg himself, that he'd lived down there
always, in the warm female bath, till even the
milk he sucked was his own, milk he'd made, first
passing it through all the loops and ligatures of
her body, the body they shared.

210.

The food is the milk of the Father, with which
children are alone nursed. The very beloved one,
he who gives us nourishment at the "care soothing breast" of the Father, that is the Logos. And
he alone, as is fitting, supplies us babes with the
milk of love, and those only are truly blessed who
suck this breast.

211.

His breasts are full of milk and his bones are moist-
ened with marrow.

212.

For those who claim male lactation is "unnatural", I would have to ask: how natural is canned formula from Nestlés or pacifiers made from petroleum byproducts? If milk production in men were truly unnatural, it wouldn't exist. The fact that it does, leads me to believe that perhaps male lactation is simply nature's back-up system. In any case, it's an interesting phenomenon.

213.

The mammary glands, the original function of which was perhaps the production of odoriferous substances, but which later became devoted solely to the secretion of milk, existed in our ancestors in a larger number than in the present human race. This is clearly shown by the fact that the human embryo normally exhibits a "hyperthelia", an excess of breasts, of which, however, two only normally undergo development; moreover, the breasts of the male, which are now in a state of arrested development, were formerly better developed, and served, like those of the female, the purpose of nourishing the offspring.

214.

With some men, after puberty, milk can be produced by squeezing the breasts; cases have been known where on their being subjected to a prolonged milking a considerable quantity of milk has been educed.

215.

Just as they are able to increase the milk yield of cows with injections of the lactogenic agent gH, the growth hormone, so it has been hypothesized that I could very possibly become a milk-producing mammary gland with the appropriate stimulation.

216.

The three Luonnotars are deities in Finnish
mythology who appear... in the songs on the
origin of iron, in which it is described how their
milk was allowed by them to run into the earth,
one dripping forth black milk, the second white,
the third blood-red; the first giving birth to
smithy-iron, the second to steel, and the third
to refuse iron.

217.

If any lips
Sought whiter draughts, with dipping finger-tips
They pressed the sod, and gushing from the ground
Came springs of milk.

218.

... in some women it flows not only from the
nipples but at diverse parts of the breasts, even
from the armpits.

219.

A time will come
To cast aside our props
Forsake
The vertical
Slump down upon the breast
As if made drunk by milk
To be suckled
By the hard pavement
Warmed at your bosom,
Cold, unyielding mother

220.

A German company has patented "nocturnal
milk", which it claims contains levels of the sleep
hormone melatonin that are 25 times higher than
that found in normal milk.

Scientific studies have shown that milk taken
from cows at night contains much higher levels

of melatonin than milk produced during the day.

221.

Night as the mingling of those "kissing cousins", birth and death. As the recumbent turns on his side, drawing up his knees, a cradle begins to tremor; as the tremor becomes a rocking, bits of yellowish froth appear, isles of conception in the endlessness of non-existence. Before we were / After we are: reciprocal postings, sped on by sleep.

222.

That evening he got all the morphia pills there were, and took them downstairs. Carefully he crushed them to powder.

"What are you doing?" said Annie.

"I s'll put 'em in her night milk."

Then they both laughed together like two conspiring children. On top of all their horror flicked this little sanity.

Nurse did not come that night to settle Mrs. Morel down. Paul went up with the hot milk in a feeding-cup. It was nine o'clock.

223.

The black Madonnas are manifestations of the ancient goddesses in her form as Isis, Demeter and Cybele. She represents the black poisonous prima materia. Cybele, the wife of Cronos, mother of the gods of Olympus is also known as Rhea, whose name means fluid. This too is a property of the prima materia.

224.

After experience of the untranquil muse one may move on to the Black Goddess—for black is positive in the East and stands for wisdom. Can a white muse become a black one, or must it be another muse? That is difficult...

225.

He smiled and said that nothing is black or white,
that whiteness is often a blackness that hides
itself and blackness is sometimes a whiteness
that's been hid.

226.

Material imagination, which always has a demi-
urgic tonality, would create all white matter from
dark matter and overcome the entire history of
blackness.

227.

the emerald day
with its shepherd of the black light
and the eternal mothers of the black milk
turn
in the acts of light.

228.

Black milk of daybreak we drink it at nightfall /
we drink it at noon in the morning we drink it
at night / drink it and drink it

229.

Whatever is soft, good, loveable and tender will
become black. Milk will be black, sugar, rice, the
sky, doves, hope will be black—the Opera as well,
where we'll go in our black Rolls, to bow to black
kings and listen to brass music under chandeliers
of black crystal.

230.

…and upon their lips the curdled milk of a million
black slave mammies' withered dugs, a treacher-
ous and fluid knowledge of our being, imbibed at
our source and now regurgitated foul upon us.

231.

I will be black as blackness can—
The blacker the mantle, the mightier the man!
For blackness was ancient ere whiteness began.
I am daubing God in night,
I am swabbing Hell in White:
I am the Smoke King
I am black.

232.

As Jean-Paul Sartre says, "we must invent the
heart of things if we wish one day to discover it.
Audiberti informs us about milk in speaking of
its secret blackness. But for Jules Renard, milk is
hopelessly white, since it is only what it seems
to be."

233.

The idea is that on the appearance of the totally
black aeroplane, which will have a small white
circle on its left wing, she is to rise up into the air
with a daring leap and then fly towards her real
life, which she has yet to discover but has sometimes sensed.

234.

You should know
Because they were the sons of Mars
Without fear
They drank the milk not meant for them.

235.

Perhaps Looking-glass milk isn't good to drink.

236.

...if anyone could synthesize "looking-glass milk"
made from molecules that were mirror images
of those that existed naturally, it would almost
certainly not be good to drink. Because such milk
may contain "anti-matter", the encounter "might

lead to a loud bang and to the total transformation of our heroine into radiant energy".

237.

…since both semen and milk (or male semen and
female semen) are extracts of blood and function
independently, they are competitive and mutu-
ally destructive; their interaction is potentially
dangerous, like the coming together of matter
and anti-matter. Semen and milk do not attract
each other, as true opposites would (such as Yin
and Yang), but repel each other, since they are so
much alike in form (white fluids expressed from a
"swollen" protrusion on the body) and function.

238.

"A few months ago, for some reason, it became a
joke on the alt-right to talk about drinking milk",
someone who knew Mike E. as a child told me. On
Twitter, "his bio said, 'Lactose tolerant'—as code
for, you know, white power. But the funny thing
was, anyone who knew him knew that any expo-
sure to dairy would make him sick."

239.

Around two-thirds of the planet has a reduced
ability to digest lactose after infancy (though
that figure is much lower for people of European
extraction). Mark Kurlansky, the author of a recent
history, *Milk! A 10,000-Year Food Fracas*, describes
the fact that many adults drink milk as a "defiance
of a basic rule of nature".

240.

There's little disputing that humans have diffi-
culty digesting dairy products. As much as 70% of
humans are dairy intolerant. This rises to close to
100% in some countries, meaning that there are
whole populations who get all the calcium they
need from plant foods. Were the milk lobby to be

believed, these people would all be suffering from poor bone health. In fact, rates of osteoporosis and hip fractures are highest in the countries with the greatest milk consumption.

241.

Growing up, Marielle Williamson was grossed out by milk. What she learned about animal agriculture made her uncomfortable. Why, she wondered, were we consuming the breast milk of another animal?

But when the 17-year-old tried to distribute literature sharing her views promoting nondairy milk at her Los Angeles high school, she says, administrators responded that it wasn't allowed unless she extolled the virtues of cow's dairy, too. ... The directive felt like a violation of her First Amendment rights. So she sued the school district and the U.S. Department of Agriculture, which oversees federal school meals policy.

[...] The USDA says schools "must not directly or indirectly restrict the sale or marketing of fluid milk at any time or in any place on school premises or at any school-sponsored event", and school nutrition manuals admonish that "program operators are not to promote or offer water or any other beverage as an alternative selection to fluid milk in their reimbursable meal throughout the food service area".

242.

With the aid of your fortifying milk, my intellect developed rapidly and took on immense proportions amid the ravishing lucidity which you bestow as a gift on all those who sincerely love you. Arithmetic! Algebra! Geometry! Awe-inspiring trinity! Luminous triangle! He who has not known you is a fool!

243.

The child poised on the threshold of a door in a
desert is also the ghost going the other way; they
are one action immortalized by a single position
towards the world: *not there.*

244.

If he asks for a kiss, kiss him.
If he asks where he is, say *gone.*

245.

The French physiologist Charles Richet coined
the term "ectoplasm" in 1894 to describe the
fluid that reportedly exuded from medium
Eusapia Palladino during séances. Mediums and
their promoters claimed the pseudo-scientific
term to name the greasy, white and sometimes
luminous substance they believed was a
manifestation of spirits.

246.

Slime can soak up any number of metaphys-
ical preconceptions and hold them in sticky
suspension. In the early 20th century, the
spiritualist movement picked up on ideas
about "cellular slime" to ground its meta-
physical claims. The "milky-white emissions"
of ectoplasm that showed up beautifully in
photographs convinced figures like Arthur
Conan Doyle that the spirit world could tangi-
bly intersect with our own. [Susanne] Wedlich
mentions props such as "fluttering gauze",
but doesn't explain that the production of
ectoplasm was often intensely visceral. The
medium's medium was cheesecloth, sometimes fisted into a tight ball and swallowed,
to be regurgitated in a clotted white string
steeped in gastric juices.

247.

...mysterious magical phlegm... made of the very
stuff of imagination itself. If one shaped this stuff
in three dimensions, it could be anything, yet this
violet ectoplasmic mental liquid must only exist
in the fourth dimension. It seemed possible to
suppose that one might pierce the other dimension and have this fluid come boiling out.

248.

And the point in the spectrum
where all lights become one,
is white and white is not no-colour,
as we were told as children,
but all colour;
where the flames mingle
and the wings meet, when we gain
the arc of perfection,
we are satisfied, we are happy,
we begin again.

249.

Note. 6 July [1916]. The Juventus [age of youth]
experiment must be regarded as absurdly
successful. I have all the symptoms of sixteen
and even earlier—great physical restlessness and
appetite for hard, athletic work—also the vague
aspirations and heedlessness of time—utter
disinclination for mental work, too, as at that
age. Further, I seem to have created in my aura all
the conditions of my own youth. I spend the day
playing at camping out; I sail a canoe, I explore
islands, I build breakwaters, etc. etc. I am living
almost entirely on milk, yet I have no tendency
to get fat, have indeed got much thinner. But the
mental lassitude and devil-may-careishness is
very marked indeed. Writing a letter is a bore. I
have also quite the boy's sex feeling. I think it is
as well I only did six operations, or I might have
wanted a wet-nurse and a toy train!

250.

McPhister: It would be amusing if his body began
to get younger and yours began to age. He certainly isn't as ill as he ought to be.
Arthur 2: He takes great care of himself. And of
me. He's so infernally temperate. He drinks nothing but milk until dinner time—milk—glasses of
milk!

251.

My son Pepi, so she said,
Take my breast that thou mayest drink, so she said;
So that thou livest (again), so that thou becomest
    small (again), so she said…

252.

I died. Deader and deader.
"Little joke corpse!" Yeah, I
shrank beyond belief…

253.

I became small, my leg became a little leg, my
hand a little hand, my persona a little persona,
my being a little being, my oeuvre a little oeuvre,
my body a little body…

254.

we say *congratulations, you're a boy again!*
we give him a durag, a bowl, a second chance.

we send him off to wander for a day
or ever, let him pick his new name.

255.

He goes back to the only original food which is
given to the innocent baby and which can help
him to grow up into a new life or a new world.

256.

I'm in the milk, and the milk's in me!

257.

The last affirmation of the mystic is "A kid I have fallen into milk". It occurs after "Thou shalt be God instead of Mortal". The question remains— what was the exact ritual of the falling into milk? ... Did the neophyte actually fall into a bath of milk...?

258.

The stage is an empty room and then the Buful Peoples start popping out in baby faces saying "Here Me Is" and shooting the audience with projection guns. Thousands of fans went mad, put on diapers and rushed through the streets shitting and pissing themselves as they screamed out: "HERE ME IS" "HERE ME IS" "HERE ME IS".

259.

A river of milk flowed in and out and around him. He floated down the milk river toward the rest of his life.

260.

The day when milk drinking was considered effeminate or juvenile has long since passed and the term "milk-sop" is no longer one of derision, but of admiration. Men like Jack Dempsey, Gene Tunney and Charles A. Lindbergh are all said to be heavy milk drinkers.

261.

Might they one day become more feminine with the aid of this drink? At present they are too muscular, much too strong.

262.

Milksop: a man lacking courage and other qualities deemed manly. A piece of bread sopped in milk. A soft, effeminate, girlish man, one who is devoid of manliness: a term of contempt.

263.

Caspar Milquetoast is a fictional character
created by H. T. Webster for his comic strip 'The
Timid Soul'. [...] The character's name is derived
from a bland and fairly inoffensive food, milk
toast, [...] an appropriate food for someone with
a weak or "nervous" stomach.

[...] the term milquetoast came into general
usage in American English to mean "weak and
ineffectual". [...] it typically indicates someone
of an unusually meek, bland, soft or submissive
nature, [...] easily overlooked, written off, [...]
overly sensitive, timid, indecisive or cowardly.

264.

In *The Metamorphosis*, Gregor's sister offers
the insect what she thought was her brother's
favorite food:

"By the door he first noticed what had really
lured him there: it was the smell of something
to eat. A bowl stood there, filled with sweetened
milk, in which swam tiny pieces of white bread.
He almost laughed with joy, for he now had a
much greater hunger than in the morning, and
he immediately dipped his head almost up to and
over his eyes down into the milk. But he soon
drew it back again in disappointment, not just
because it was difficult for him to eat on account
of his delicate left side—he could eat only if his
entire panting body worked in a coordinated
way—but also because the milk, which otherwise
was his favorite drink and which his sister had
certainly placed there for that reason, did not
appeal to him at all. He turned away from the
bowl almost with aversion and crept back into
the middle of the room."

This bowl of milk toast—the epitome of wholesome dairy fare—is nauseating to the insect.

265.

He had led such a disgruntled existence that he had begun to enjoy the spectacle of a tumbler of water being filled, emptied, and filled again. A slow smile of gratification flashed into the air. It seemed to emanate from his chin, but he knew this was unlikely. He was evidently upset. He tumbled forward into a beaker of milk. This was his last chance. He grabbed his legs, and tucking them up under his collar, he rolled quietly into the harbour.

266.

Harriet (the stronger puppet): I hope you are beginning to think about our milk.
Rhoda (after a pause): Well, I'm not.
Harriet: Now what's the matter with you? You're not going to have a visitation from our dead, are you?
Rhoda: I don't have visitations this winter because I'm too tired to love even our dead. Anyway, I'm disgusted with the world.
Harriet: Just mind your business. I mind mine and I am thinking about our milk.
Rhoda: I'm so tired of being sad. I'd like to change.

267.

... It is not enough to be killed, you must be torn to pieces or burnt to ashes. Above all you must utterly forget your past life.

268.

dead is the safest I've ever been,
I've never been so alive.

269.

18 year-old girl
3 year-old boy:
he pees & shits
in his pajamas,

has to be carried off
& tucked into bed.
sleeps until midnight,
then it's milk he wants.
whippity-whap!
(2 little slaps),—
"I'm your *wife*,
not your *mother!*"

270.

"Do you want it pasteurized?"
"No, just up to my mouth would be fine."

271.

Does milk want to express itself through me? Am
I a breast or teat? An udder? "I is an udder." Am I
allowed to crack jokes? Who's in charge here?

272.

Italy's Supreme Court has ordered a plastic
surgeon to pay 122m lire (£23,000) damages to a
woman who as a result of a bungled breast operation lost her nipples, her career and her husband.
[...]
In Italy, a country renowned for its obsession
with mothers and madonnas, where even seri-
ous magazines regularly have topless women on
their covers, the ruling means that to damage
a woman's breasts is tantamount to defacing a
Baroque fountain or scratching a Renaissance
painting. "I had one of the most beautiful cleav-
ages in the history of cinema", Gina Lollobrigida
once said of herself. Now even offscreen bosoms
are to be respected as works of art, with a mone-
tary value.

273.

The female body, even at its best, is very defective
in form; it has harsh curves and very clumsily
distributed masses; compared to it the average

milk-jug, or even cuspidor, is a thing of intelligent and gratifying design.

274.

See what a vigorous body I have! … See the muscles upon my arms, look at my breasts, round and unripe, not like a woman. You might almost say that yours are swelling with drops of milk!

275.

… only through the patient's numerous associations and his statement that a voice emerged from inside of a breastlike cloud was it possible to ascertain that, in effect, the breast concealed the percept of a face.

276.

… I did not, like other infants, come crying into the world, but perked up, and laughed immediately in my mother's face. And there is no reason I should envy Jove for having a she-goat for his nurse, since I was more creditably suckled by two jolly nymphs; the name of the first drunkenness, one of Bacchus's offspring, the other ignorance, the daughter of Pan; both which you may here behold among several others of my train and attendants, whose particular names, if you would fain know, I will give you in short. This, who goes with a mincing gait, and holds up her head so high, is Self-Love. She that looks so spruce, and makes such a noise and bustle, is Flattery. That other, which sits hum-drum, as if she were half asleep, is called Forgetfulness. She that leans on her elbow, and sometimes yawningly stretches out her arms, is Laziness. This, that wears a plighted garland of flowers, and smells so perfumed, is Pleasure. The other, which appears in so smooth a skin, and pampered-up flesh, is Sensuality. She that stares so wildly, and rolls about her eyes, is Madness. As to those two gods

whom you see playing among the lasses the name
of the one is Intemperance, the other Sound Sleep.
By the help and service of this retinue I bring all
things under the verge of my power, lording it
over the greatest kings and potentates.

277.

I appear with the face of an adult and the body
of a baby girl, in the arms of my nana... From
her nipples falls milk as from the sky... I came
out looking like such a little girl and she so
strong and so saturated with providence, that
it made me long to sleep.

278.

And while in my heart I was outraged that Mama
too wanted to force me to eat, my eyes fell to her
bosom, and when she insisted, "But why don't
you want the apples I buy you?" I knew what I
was yearning for so desperately and I was able to
bring out, "Because the apples you buy are food
for grown-ups and I want real apples, Mama's
apples, like those," and I pointed to Mama's
breasts.

   She got up at once, went to get a magnificent
apple, cut a piece and gave it to me, saying, "Now,
Mama is going to feed her little Renée. It is time
to drink the good milk from Mama's apples." She
put the piece in my mouth, and with my eyes
closed, my head against her breast, I ate, or rather
drank, my milk.

279.

We learn that Boudet, for reasons that are never
given, had "for a long time been haunted by
the idea of artificially fertilizing a woman with
the pollen of a flower". These attempts always
fail, until he reads of an extremely fertile Texan
woman, called Catherine Seyeux, who has given
birth to 45 children. He writes to her, offering

a magnificent sum for her participation in his efforts to produce a hybrid *enfant-fleur*. Catherine agrees, and sets off for France. Boudet's very first attempt to make her pregnant with pollen is successful, and the result is Bertha...

[...]

Bertha, we are assured, is quite happy as long as she is in the sun, but exhibits discontent if a shadow falls on her. She lies on a soft rack that has been especially constructed for her, and which is painted the same pinkish colour as her skin. Most unsettling of all is Boudet's demonstration of her being breast-fed: despite her frailty, Bertha is able to seize her mother's breast in her small hands and guide it to her lips, allowing the intrepid scientist and his guests to watch, through her transparent exterior, the milk pass down her oesophagus and into her stomach.

280.

After 25 years of research, Dr. Paul Shattock... has developed a theory that particular proteins in [milk and wheat] lead to autism, which affects about one in 1,000 children. The proteins interfere with the neurons inside the developing brain, leaving children withdrawn and uninterested in the world around them.

281.

In later years Wain's harmless eccentricities—such as drinking milk from a saucer at parties—multiplied, and he was admitted to a Napsbury Mental Hospital with schizophrenia.

282.

Hard, hard this cat-world.
On the stream Vicissitude
Our milk flowed lewd.

We'll cry, we'll cry,

We'll cry the more
And wet the floor...

283.

Two of [William] Wegman's works reference
milk's potability and relation to the body.
Drinking Milk (1971) shows two scenes in which
a man apparently consumes milk through a
straw in his navel. The contraction of the abdo-
men mimics the effect of suction by the mouth
and cheeks. The resemblance of the straw to the
umbilical cord testifies to the infantile regression
involved in the adult's consumption of milk. The
gesture signals an obstinate persistence in maternal attachment, although not, in this case, to the
breast, and thus alludes to an even more primal
refusal of parturition.

284.

[Francis Battalia, seventeenth-century stone-
eater] "was borne with two stones in one hand
and one in the other; who as soone as he was
borne having the breast offered unto him, refused
to suck"; when he also refused any other nourishment a doctor was summoned and told of
the peculiarity of the baby's birth. The physician
advised that the child be given small pebbles in
liquid, which he happily devoured, and for thirty
years he ate almost nothing else.

285.

For why may not the mother be naught, a peevish,
drunken flirt, a waspish, choleric slut, a crazed
piece, a fool (as many mothers are), unsound, as
soon as the nurse? There is more choice of nurses
than mothers; and therefore, except the mother be
most virtuous, staid, a woman of excellent good
parts, and of a sound complexion, I would have
all children in such cases committed to discreet
strangers.

286.

... I created pictures of watchful, buzzing mothers
who shed their shells on the trunks of trees like
locusts. On cue, I turned the enormous, newly
hatched insects into nuns at his parochial school.
I made roses grow from the ends of their fingers.
I watched them walk into their students' dreams
on a beam of light.

287.

"Zuckerman finally realized that his mother had
been his only love." When she dies, in Florida,
he takes away from her effects an old book of
hers called *Your Baby's Care*; on the page headed
"Feeding", which prescribes emptying the breasts
by hand every 24 hours, he finds a stain that he
believes to have been left by a drop of her milk,
expressed in 1933, and he closes his eyes and puts
his tongue to the dry page. Adult infantilism can
go no further.

288.

You have weaned me
too soon
you must nurse me again

289.

When the child has to be weaned the mother
blackens her breast, but her eyes rest just as
lovingly on the child. The child believes it is the
breast that has changed, but that the mother is
unchanged. And why does she blacken her breast?
Because, she says, it would be a shame that it
should seem delicious when the child must not
get it.

290.

The secret fantasy of poisoned milk, of nourishment that kills, originates early in life when the
decisive separation between child and mother

takes place. The elevation of this fantasy, which is occasionally encountered clinically, to the status of myth for a whole culture indicates the intensity of inner conflict associated with this separation...

291.

The hopeless wish for his own breasts leaves ineradicable traces on the boy's development and on the formation of his character. He desires throughout his life to avenge himself on women for possessing something which he lacks. Till the end of his days, the female breast will inspire in him both a desire for ownership and a rage at his own shortcomings in not developing breasts himself. The first sentiment usually translates into a need to touch or suck women's breasts, and the bigger the better. The second sentiment results in self-contempt, which is sometimes displaced into acts of violence against women, with breasts specifically targeted for retaliation.

292.

Did the voice tell you to use the ice-pick?
No.
Did you hear the voice all the time you were hitting her?
Yes. Loud. Kill... kill.
Where did you stab her?
All over.
Any special place?
Breasts.
Why her breasts?
Make milk.
Did you want milk?
Don't know.

293.

The tenderest infant, yet imbibing nutrition from the mamilla of maternal love, and the agonized

mother herself, alike await the stroke of the
relentless tomahawk.

294.

In 'The Face-Breast Equation' he offers several
additional clinical examples. The first concerns
an ophthalmologist, the eldest of eight children,
whose mother weaned his siblings by painting
her nipples with a mixture of vinegar and char-
coal in order to bring about revulsion in the child.
His presenting symptoms included the fact that
"when he operated on a patient's eye with the
assistance of a female attendant, he was under
tremendous tension, which he attributed to the
fear that his hand might slip and that he might
thrust the knife forcefully into the patient's orbit".
Speculating as to "why this symptom was present
only in the presence of his nurse, … he realized
that while he had only been consciously aware
of his wish to fondle her breasts, actually he felt
strong aggressive impulses against her".

295.

We had effects in there that I myself was literally
afraid of: When we french-fried that girl's face…
when we cut off the girl's nipples (and out of one
came milk and out of the other chocolate milk).
I felt that was the ultimate in black humour,
but there were those in the audience who didn't
understand… and didn't see—well, they saw
what I intended, but they thought it was a dese-
cration to have chocolate milk come out of a…
[laughter].

296.

It doesn't end
When the world
says a relieved farewell to the white man
As he goofs off to colonise the Milky Way

It continues, it continues.

297.

The large pendulous breast was seen for many centuries as a sign of the outré and primitive. Hermann Heinrich Ploss's ethnographic study of "woman", first published in 1885, refers to the breasts of the "black" race as resembling a goat's udder. The anthropologist Hans Friedenthal was even to claim, in his 1925 essay 'Muttersprache und Mutterbrust', that the structure of primitive languages was formed by the pressure of the savage mother's breast, referring to nurture patterns among "Hottentots and Bushmen" and to the "strange sounds of their languages which is in harmony with the club-shaped breasts of the mothers which shaped the lips of the nursing child".

298.

The nineteenth century took its breasts very seriously, or so I suspect—I can't get into a library to check. I am thinking of those references I found particularly exciting or unsettling as a child. The heroes of *King Solomon's Mines*, for example, as they toil up Sheba's left Breast (a mountain), tortured by thirst. The chapter is called 'Water! Water!' and comes from a time when you were allowed to be so obvious it hurt. "Heavens, how we did drink!" These extinct volcanoes are "inexpressibly solemn and overpowering". In the attempt to describe their "extraordinary grandeur and beauty... language seems to fail" him, despite which the narrator staggers on until "as though to veil the majestic sight from our curious eyes, strange mists and clouds gathered and increased around them, till presently we could only trace their pure and gigantic outline swelling ghost-like through the fleecy envelope". In a desperate drama of hunger and satiation our heroes climb

through lava and snow up to the hillock of the
enormous, freezing nipple. There they find a cave,
occupied by a dead man (What?! What?!), and in
this cave one of their party also dies: Ventvögel,
a "Hottentot" whose "snubnose" had enabled
him, when still alive, to sniff out water (we don't
want to know).

So far, so infantile.

299.

In Papua New Guinea Pidgin, milk and breast (or
udder) are SUSU, which also means pus. SUSU
is also "a deep, narrow fish of milky whiteness,
about fifteen inches long, found under reefs
and belonging to the trevally family" (Murphy).
Perhaps from Malay, in which milk is also SUSU.
Cajun, likewise, calls a type of fish SAC A LAIT
(bag of milk). In Swahili, milk is MAZIWA, related
to ZIWA, a woman's breast (there is another word
for an animal's udder). The primary meaning of
ZIWA is "lake, pond, marsh, pool"...

300.

But more, more about the breast itself—all my life
I've dreamed on breasts (and of course thighs, but
now we're talking of breasts, hold your Venus,
we're talking about Mars, and your water, we're
talking about milk)

301.

... the whole breast is so spongy that if a woman
in drinking happen to swallow a hair, she gets
a pain in her breast, which ailment is called a
"trichia"; and the pain lasts till the hair either find
its own way out or be sucked out with the milk.

302.

Our sages declare that there is a kind of death...
as easy as drawing a hair out of milk, and this is
called the death of the kiss.

303.

Pliny the Elder claims "Chilo" (full name Lucius
Fabius Cilo Septiminus Catinius Acilianus Lepidus
Fulcinianus) perished from choking on a single
hair in a draught of milk.

304.

Sure, we have complex thoughts, and these
convenient, opposable thumbs. Yet sooner or
later our bosoms will betray us, because when it
comes to how we nourish our offspring, humans
and other mammals are the same. That's part of
the reason human attitudes toward breast milk
have always been so complicated: we can strap
our breasts down in sports bras or dress them in
sexy lingerie, but at the end of the day, we're still
walking around with udders on our chests.

305.

If you're a parent with young children,
you've likely encountered a sanctimommy.
Sanctimommies are that modern species of
sanctimonious mothers who liberally dispense
parenting advice laced with the subtext, "I'm not
saying you're a bad parent, but..." Smug in their
maternal superiority, they crusade perhaps most
vehemently against moms who choose not to
breast-feed.

   If this moralism were limited to sanctimommies, it might be written off as nothing more
than parenting blog fodder. But according to
'Lactivism', Courtney Jung's riveting exposé
of the forces that have turned the simple act
of feeding one's baby into a veritable battle-
field, "to breast-feed or not to breast-feed" has
become a question with far-reaching impli-
cations spanning medicine, politics, religion,
feminism, commerce, race and social class.

306.

The child who swallows the amnion now
      will swallow milk
   by winter. The milk

can find a use for me but not
      for my belief,
   nor yours, and it beggars the best
of our purposes.

307.

As an infant, I agree
mother's breast is best for me.
But her submission to my bent
offers more than nourishment.

Baby whales and baby bats
drink in minerals and fats,
but I absorb a paradigm
that will haunt me for all time.

Milk is why we're given lips
and why we form relationships.
What is kissing after all
but nursing that is mutual?

308.

It seems not only that the adult male becomes in
face-to-face copulation, a surrogate suckling to
the adult female by virtue of his position; but also
that the adult female becomes a surrogate suckling to the male by virtue of her behaviour, which
is that of soliciting and receiving a life-giving
liquid from an adult bodily protuberance.

309.

He is no longer the Ben that I know at all. Helen
undoes her blouse, never letting his penis rest,
sucking away on it. She takes her breasts in her
own hands, and kneads them so that drops of

milk gush from them onto Ben's pubic hair, soaking them. ...Ben is about to come in her mouth, but he wants the milk even more and he lifts her, drags her onto the sofa, so that he can suck her breasts while his hands undress her...

310.

And without waiting for an answer from Alejandro, she kissed him full on the mouth, stretched out with him under the udders of the cows, and took permanent possession of his sex. He, after gushing forth his soul in his seed, squeezed the udders and bathed the two of them in a shower of hot milk.

311.

Making good love, making good good love
Because peace is milk
Peace is milk
And the skinny, thirsty earth,
its face covered with flies
Screams like a baby

312.

...where our bodies were glued together there was flowing, out of her, over me, over the floor of the roof, flowing everywhere, some sort of obsidian liquid, something dark and glittering, with color and lights within it. After the DMT flash, after the seizure of the orgasms, after all that, this new thing shocked me to the core. What was this fluid and what was going on? I looked at it. I looked right into it, and it was the surface of my own mind reflected in front of me. Was it translinguistic matter, the living opalescent excrescence of the alchemical abyss of hyperspace, something generated by the sex act performed under such crazy conditions?

313.

Our organs nurse at our veins like infants at the breast. Blood is cellular milk. In fact, adult or aged man, whether we suck, chew, or gulp our mixture, our entire life on earth is a physiological activity at the sucking bottle of ourselves. Organically we are our own mother-and-child; and in the infinity of things, in Absolute Allness, we suck from God Himself.

314.

Toads thrive on burning cigarette ends and human milk. Some forty years ago I had to read the Letters of Junius. All I remember is that one of the royal family was "subject to the hideous suction of toads".

315.

The philosophers... would never put such a poisonous animal to a woman's breast, "were the toad not her own miracle-birth and fruit, which she had brought into the world as a monster". When it has suckled its fill, the white Mercurial woman dies, becoming the red sulphur of the philosophers. "Seek to prepare from it a medicine which may draw all the poison from your heart."

316.

Their lordships sucked the peasantry dry of their finances, but besides the fiscal sucking they carried on an infantile kind of sucking, they sucked not only their blood but also their sweet milk, and no matter how harshly and mercilessly my uncle swore at the grooms, no matter how much, like a mommy, auntie let them kiss her hands with matriarchal kindliness—neither matri-archal nor patriarchal kindliness, nor the severest of commands could quell the impression that the squire was actually the peasantry's little son, and the squire's lady—their little daughter.

317.

Haven't I always been a cannibal? As a child I
sucked my mother's breasts, draining her flesh. I
longed to taste the salt of her blood through the
salt of milk, trying to replace the blood that used
to come to me through the umbilical cord, to flow
through me like alcohol through an alcohol addict.
Maybe only those of us who remember mother's
blood become alcoholics, trying not to forget but
to remember. We started with the mother; our
basic nature stems not from the assassination of
the father but from the slow killing of the mother.

318.

... mother's milk was stiff as sand.

319.

stiff, o dairyman, in a myriad of fits

320.

Two young brothers have been promised as much
cream as they can eat after doctors suggested
that it might help their epilepsy. [...] The diet
results in the production of ketones in the body,
which interfere with the triggering of fits, but
the mechanism of their action on the brain is not
understood. It works in children but is not effec-
tive in adults.

321.

Children are very commonly subject to convul-
sions, more especially such of them as are more
than ordinarily well-nourished on rich or unusually plentiful milk from a stout nurse.

322.

Children are nourished for the Slaughter; once the
                                    Child was fed
With Milk, but wherefore now are children fed
                                    with blood?

323.

The milk "junkies" who are hooked on crime
[Headline in *The New York Post*, the article, by Pat
Smith begins]:
Juvenile delinquents drink more than twice as
much milk as normal youngsters, a startling new
survey showed today.
[It ends by quoting Alex Schauss, a psychologist
who is conducting the study]:
We never thought twice about it until a researcher
called me at home one night and said, "Alex, these
children drink way too much milk".

324.

"Is there really such a place as Putte? Where is it?"
"In the suburbs of Antwerp. A large borough.
Nothing but distilleries. The kids drink gin from
their mother's breast till it pisses out of their eyes,
then they put it back in their feeding bottles."

325.

I had... an immense desire to know what kind of
moral character belonged to the man who had
fathered such criminal eccentricity. I wagered
myself that he must be fundamentally evil. I had
enquiries made, and my instincts were gratified
by winning this psychological bet. I learned that
the monster arose regularly before dawn; that he
had brought his charwoman to ruin; and that he
drank only milk!

326.

Many respectable men have been eaten alive by
the words of their own creation, for their appetite
exceeds that of Frankenstein's healthful monster,
and I have reasons for suspecting that, like the
ferocious Scythians of old, they drink only milk.
Milk! That explains everything.

327.

And it is from them alone that all manipulators
buy their food: plasma
of the animal, human or otherwise, and that
    juice
all witch men, high or low, feed off, the
    white stuff.

328.

In *Le Tentazioni del Dottor Antonio* (The Temptation
of Dr Antonio) Dr Antonio Mazzuolo, a middle-
aged man, has taken it upon himself to be the
protector of Rome's morality from what he sees
as vice and immorality throughout the city. [...]
His anger knows no bounds when a provocative
billboard of Anita Ekberg with the tag line "drink
more milk" is put up in a park near his residence.
Little does he know how the billboard will impact
his life. Throughout the film, children are heard
singing the jingle "Bevete più latte, bevete più
latte!" ("Drink more milk!"). The image begins to
haunt him with hallucinations in which Ekberg
appears as a temptress. After his delirium culmi-
nates in throwing a spear at Ekberg's image, he is
found collapsed on top of the billboard and trans-
ported away in an ambulance to the children's
song.

329.

The 65-year-old Tamil actor Shivaji Rao Gaekwad,
better known as Rajinikanth, is one of India's
most celebrated and well-paid movie stars. For
decades, fans have regularly bathed pictures of
him in thousands of litres of milk, a sign of devo-
tion usually reserved for Hindu idols.
    With every new film Rajinikanth releases,
milk becomes so in demand in some parts of the
country that it is stolen from markets, resulting in
shortages that potentially endanger malnourished
children, officials and activists say.

330.

the smoothness, the tumescence, the milky flow
of feminine nudity anticipates a sensation of
liquid outpour, which itself opens onto death like
a window onto a courtyard.

331.

A phrase is recorded on tape, e.g. "drop salt into
milk". And the tape is formed into a loop so that
the same phrase is played over and over again…
Now if we listen to this repeated utterance, it
seems to change. We hear other words, we hear
nonsense sounds, it is difficult to believe that we
are merely listening to the same phrase over and
over.

332.

It's nice to be like a madman, mad over a single
point. Such a man sees his point everywhere and
in everything. Everything is grist for his mill.
Everything has a direct relationship to his beloved
point.

333.

…many diverse images, borrowed from very
different orders of things, may, by the convergence
of their action, direct the consciousness to the
precise point where there is a certain intuition to
be seized.

334.

…from milk, the all-too-visible substance of
scientific photography and the modern, endlessly
advertised commodity, to alcoholic spirits; to
blood, the essence that sustains spirit; to the
semen that transmits spirit; to ectoplasm, the
phantasmic substance of spirit. *Pneuma*, or
spirit, is the point at which all meanings of milk
converge.

335.
Milk, it connects
Milk it is not cum
A kind of off-white blood
Not an aftereffect
I squirt all over the sheets
My lifeforce.

336.
...the white curve on black ground we call thought...

337.
O fuck. Let the gruff bark! Go ahead. Write tough
& hard in the saddle. Shoot straight. I'm in the
movies too. Act III may be late in coming. & I'm
in the movies too. Me. Me. ME. I'm a terrible liar.
& who knows, we may yet ride together into the
innocuous sunset or the last drop of milk.

338.
...to each cask filled with this wine was added a
drop of milk from a young mother's breast and a
drop of seed from a young stallion. These lend to
the wine secret seductive powers. Whoever drinks
hereof does so at his own risk and must answer
for himself.

339.
Bachelard was probably right in seeing water
as the opposite of wine: mythically, this is true;
sociologically, today at least, less so; economic
and historical circumstances have given this part
to milk. The latter is now the true anti-wine:
[...] in the basic morphology of substances milk
is the opposite of fire by all the denseness of its
molecules, by the creamy, and therefore soothing,
nature of its spreading. Wine is mutilating, surgical, it transmutes and delivers; milk is cosmetic, it
joins, covers, restores. Moreover, its purity, asso-

ciated with the innocence of the child, is a token of strength, of a strength which is not revulsive, not congestive, but calm, white, lucid, the equal of reality. Some American films, in which the hero, strong and uncompromising, did not shrink from having a glass of milk before drawing his avenging Colt, have paved the way for this new Parsifalian myth.

...milk remains an exotic substance.

340.

...this same glass, contemplated by different beings, can be a thousand different things, because each one charges what he sees with *effectivity*; no one sees things as they are, but as his desires and his state of soul make him see.

341.

...absolute dairy visions:
Corduroy eggs, owl cheese, pipe butter,
Firing squad milk...

342.

After several minutes the bomb squad appeared, moving cautiously forward, carefully cleared the snow, and came up with the bag, which they picked up and looked inside. Inside was only a fractured glass that had apparently but not certainly been filled with milk.

Over the decades friends and family members have contributed materials to my collection for which I'm grateful. My main debt of gratitude, however, is to the authors who have contributed unwittingly, whose words I've appropriated.

Thanks to Chris Allen for proofreading and to the book's publisher and designer Colin Sackett for aiding and abetting from first to last.

Milk files, NYC, 1978

Sources

1. Lewis Carroll, 'Musings on Milk', *The Rectory Magazine*

2. Tammy Faye Bakker*

3. C. G. Jung, *Psychology and Alchemy*

4. David Sylvester

5. François Truffaut, *Hitchcock/Truffaut*

6. Edward Lear, *The Dong with a Luminous Nose*

7. Daniel Spoerri from the *Petit Echo Diététique*, no.46, June 1960, quoted in note 64, 'Corner of half-litre of Milk', in *An Anecdoted Topography of Chance*

8. John Ashbery, *How Much Longer Will I Be Able to Inhabit the Divine Sepulcher...*

9. William Carlos Williams, *The Great American Novel*, chapter one, 'The Fog'

10. Claude Levi-Strauss, *The Raw and the Cooked*

11. Francis Ponge, *The Goat*, trans. Beth Archer

12. Etymology of *mythos* in Liddell & Scott's *Greek-English Lexicon*, 1897 edition, quoted by Robert Duncan in *The Truth and Life of Myth*

13. William Carlos Williams, *The Great American Novel*, chapter one, 'The Fog'

14. Michel Serres, *The Five Senses: A Philosophy of Mingled Bodies*

15. Anne Enright, 'My Milk', the *London Review of Books*, 5 Oct. 2000

16. James Rampton, *The Independent on Sunday*, 18 Nov. 1990

17. Shakespeare, *Henry VI, Part 1*

18. Gaston Bachelard, *Water and Dreams*

19. *The Hermetic and Alchemical Writings of Paracelsus*, vol.1, Hermetic Chemistry, ed. Arthur Edward Waite

20. Witold Gombrowicz, *Ferdydurke*

21. Joan Didion, *Play It as It Lays*

22. Jean-Paul Sartre, *Words*

23. William James, Lecture IX, 'Conversion', in *The Varieties of Religious Experience*

24. Ted Berrigan, quoted in *Milk Quarterly*, Fall, 1974

25. James Hillman, 'Senex and Puer', in *Puer Papers*

26. Erich Neumann, *The Great Mother*

27. Bernadette Mayer, *Ice Cube Epigrams*

28. Christoph Asendorf, *Batteries of Life*

29. Christopher Morley

30. Antonin Artaud

31. Robert M. Coates, *The Eater of Darkness*

32. Ettore Sottsass talking to Ian Phillips in the *Independent Magazine*, July 2002

33. Thom Gunn, *The Annihilation of Nothing*

34. Leonardo da Vinci, *A Treatise on Painting*

35. James Hillman, 'Puer Wounds and Ulysses' Scar', in *Puer Papers*

36. Italo Calvino, *If on a Winter's Night a Traveller*

37. Wallace Stevens, *The Glass of Water*

38. Gaston Bachelard, re. *The Egg in the Landscape* a prose-poem by André Pieyre de Mandiargues

39. Witold Gombrowicz, *Ferdydurke*

40. Helen Shaw, quoting either James Grissom or Tennessee Williams in 'The Interview Artist', *The New Yorker*, 12 June 2023

41. August Strindberg, *Sleepwalking Nights on Wide-awake Days*

---

* Former wife of disgraced televangelist Jim Bakker who was sentenced in 1989 to forty-five years in prison on twenty-four counts of fraud and conspiracy (he served five). After sentencing, Jim Bakker "lay in bed for a month with his bible in his hand, begging God not to let him lose his mind completely. The doctor ordered a diet of milk and cream. 'You can't imagine how much milk is in a glass of milk', observed Tammy."—*The National Enquirer*

42. Alice Spawls, 'List Your Enemies', a review of *Hot Milk* by Deborah Levy, *London Review of Books*, 16 June 2016

43. Anne Enright, 'My Milk', *London Review of Books*, 5 Oct. 2000

44. Michel Thévoz, 'The Sorcery of Words in the Body of the Text', trans. Allen S. Weiss, *Art & Text* 27, 1988

45. Vesna Goldsworthy, *Chernobyl Strawberries*

46. Simone de Beauvoir, *The Second Sex*

47. Anne Enright, 'My Milk', *London Review of Books*, 5 Oct. 2000

48. Holbrook Jackson, *The Anatomy of Bibliomania*

49. James Hillman, 'Senex and Puer', *Puer Papers*

50. Isaiah 28:9

51. Heb. v. 13–14

52. Michael Slackman, 'Egyptians Recoil as Religious Edicts Swell', *New York Times*, 24 June 2007

53. *Living Russian: a complete language course*, Living Language

54. Ursula K. Le Guin, *The Left Hand of Darkness*

55. Jane Ellen Harrison, *Themis*

56. René Crevel, 'Are You Crazy?', in *Atlas* III, trans. David Gascoyne

57. Harold Bayley, *The Lost Language of Symbolism: An Inquiry into the Origin of Certain Letters, Words, Names, Fairy-Tales, Folklore, and Mythologies*

58. Unica Zürn, *The House of Illnesses*, trans. Malcolm Green

59. Anna Kavan, *Ice*

60. Henry David Thoreau, *Walden*, chapter eighteen: Conclusion

61. Nelson Hilton, 'Before the Milk of the Word: Nipple-Eyes', chapter two of *Lexis Complexes*

62. Witold Gombrowicz, *Ferdydurke*

63. Joseph Campbell, *The Hero With a Thousand Faces*, quoting Isaiah, 66: 10–12

64. Sir Walter Raleigh, *The Passionate Man's Pilgrimage*

65. Marghanita Laski, *Ecstasy: A Study of some Secular and Religious Experiences*

66. Joseph Campbell, *The Hero With a Thousand Faces*

67. Henri Bosco, *L'Antiquaire*, quoted by Gaston Bachelard in *The Poetics of Space*, trans. Maria Jolas

68. Barbara O'Brien, *Operators and Things: The Inner Life of a Schizophrenic*

69. Hans Bellmer, *The Anatomy of the Image*

70. Wallace Stevens, *Notes Toward a Supreme Fiction*

71. Ian Hunt, re. *Cyclops*, a video/performance/installation by Brian Catling at the South London Gallery, 1996

72. Paul Metcalf, *I-57*

73. Kenneth Hayes, *Milk and Melancholy*

74. Wyndham Lewis, *Blast*, no.1

75. Theodore Roethke, *The Lost Son*

76. Saint-John Perse, *And You, Seas*

77. James Merrill, *Lost in Translation*

78. Uno Holmberg, *The Tree of Life*

79. Anne Enright, 'My Milk', *London Review of Books*, 5 Oct. 2000

80. Nelson Hilton, 'Before the Milk of the Word: Nipple-Eyes', chapter two of *Lexis Complexes*

81. Roger Gilbert-Lecomte, 'Notes for a Coming Attraction', in *Black Mirror*, trans. David Rattray

82. Ezra Pound, *Canto LXXIV*

83. William Carlos Williams, *Marianne Moore*

84. Michel Leiris, *Aurora*, trans. Terry Hale

85. Jacques-Emile Blanche on 'Le Bœuf sur le Toit' by Jean Cocteau, from *Comedia*, 21 Feb. 1920, trans. Nancy E. Nes, *The Drama Review*, vol.16, no.3, Sept. 1972

86. Elizabeth Smart, *By Grand Central Station I Sat Down and Wept*

87. Danez Smith, *Don't Call Us Dead*

88. Gaston Bachelard, *On Poetic Imagination and Reverie*

89. Shakespeare, *A Midsummer Night's Dream*, Act V, Scene 1

90. Rudolf Arnheim, *Art and Visual Perception*

91. Joanne H. Stroud, foreword to *Water and Dreams* by Gaston Bachelard

92. Sigmund Freud, *The Interpretation of Dreams*

93. David Antin, 'the sociology of art', from *talking at the boundaries*

94. Samuel Beckett, *Proust*

95. Walt Whitman, *Song of Myself*

96. Travis Jeppesen, *The Object*

97. John Cage, *Lecture on Nothing*

98. Melanie Jackson & Esther Leslie, *Deeper in the Pyramid*

99. Wendy Doniger O'Flaherty, *Women, Androgynes, and Other Mythical Beasts*

100. Gertrude Stein, *Next: Life & Letters of Marcel Duchamp*

101. Erik Satie, *A Musician's Life*

102. Edmund Burke

103. Michael Pollan, *The Botany of Desire: A Plant's-Eye View of the World*

104. J. M. Coetzee, 'Why we worry about meat', *The Independent*, 10 Dec. 1995

105. Italo Calvino, *If on a Winter's Night a Traveller*

106. *redjuice.co.uk* (accessed April 2023)

107. Anne Carson, *The Glass Essay*

108. Samuel J. Crumbine & James A. Tobey, *The Most Nearly Perfect Food: The Story of Milk*

109. Paracelsus, *De Sensibus*

110. Edward Davidson, quoted by Sidney Kaplan in his Introduction to *The Narrative of Arthur Gordon Pym of Nantucket* by Edgar Allan Poe

111. Lorine Niedecker, *The Years Go By*

112. Jack Spicer, *After Lorca*

113. William Carlos Williams, *The Descent*

114. John Osborne, *Luther*

115. Thomas Pynchon, *Gravity's Rainbow*

116. Henri Michaux, *Miserable Miracle*, trans. Louise Varese

117. Brad Fox, *The Bathysphere Book, Effects of the Luminous Ocean Depths*

118. Michel Leiris, *Aurora*, trans. Terry Hale

119. Georges Bataille, *Eroticism*

120. Charles-Augustin Sainte-Beuve, *Vie, poésies et pensées de Joseph Delorme*, trans. John R. Clark

121. Gertrude Stein, *Before the Flowers of Friendship Faded Friendship Faded*

122. John Barth, *Night-Sea Journey*

123. Charles Simic, *Return to a Place Lit by a Glass of Milk*

124. Kenneth Hayes, *Milk and Melancholy*

125. Anaïs Nin, *Collages*

126. Margaret Naumburg, *Dynamically Oriented Art Therapy: Its Principles and Practice*

127. Gertrude Stein, *Before the Flowers of Friendship Faded Friendship Faded*

128. Extract from book four of *Fragments from the Estate of a Young Physicist* by Johann Wilhelm Ritter (trans. Malcolm Green)

129. Ludwig Wittgenstein (citing Philipp Otto Runge), *Remarks on Colour*

130. *The Hermetic and Alchemical Writings of Paracelsus*, vol.1, Hermetic Chemistry, ed. Arthur Edward Waite

131. Mark Leyner, 'I was an infinitely hot and dense dot', in the collection *My Cousin, My Gastroenterologist*

132. John Lanchester, *The Debt to Pleasure*

133. Clifton Fadiman, *Any Number Can Play*

134. E. Newton Harvey, *A History of Luminescence, From the Earliest Times Until 1900*

135. Stassa Edwards, 'A Study in Butter', *mentalfloss.com/article/82030/show-tell-study-butter*

136. Edith Sitwell, *Ass-Face*

137. Samuel J. Crumbine & James A. Tobey, *The Most Nearly Perfect Food: The Story of Milk*

138. Anon, *Aristotle's Masterpiece, or, The Secrets of Nature Displayed*

139. Sylvia Plath, *Poem for a Birthday*

140. G. S. Kirk, *Myth, Its Meaning and Functions in Ancient and Other Cultures*

141. 'Man made myths about nature', *The Reader's Digest Book of Strange Stories, Amazing Facts*

142. G. S. Kirk, *Myth, Its Meaning and Functions in Ancient and Other Cultures*

143. Dylan Thomas, part VII of *Altarwise by Owl-Light*

144. Bob Dylan, *Ballad of a Thin Man*

145. Lonnie Johnson, *Jersey Belle Blues*

146. Jean Cocteau, *Angel Heurtebise*, trans. Kristin Prevallet

147. Richard Wilbur, *Epistemology*

148. Angela Carter, *American Ghosts & Old World Wonders*

149. Russell Edson, 'How the Bull Lost His Mind', in *See Jack*

150. Joyce McDougall & Serge Lebovici, *Dialogue with Sammy: Psychoanalytical Contribution to the Understanding of Child Psychosis*

151. Benjamin Péret, *Honest Folk*, trans. Ruthven Todd

152. José Kozer, 'White ambiguity of hours', in the collection *Prójimos*, trans. Ammiel Alcalay

153. *New York Times*, Aug. 1997

154. Ogden Nash, *The Cow*

155. Henri Frankfort, *Kingship and the Gods*

156. G. K. Chesterton, *The Man Who Was Thursday*

157. Lewis Carroll, *The Rectory Magazine*

158. Ben Katchor, *The Dairy Restaurant*

159. Paul Farley & Michael Symmons Roberts, *Edgelands: Journeys into England's True Wilderness*

160. Katie Stout, *Udder Table*

161. *Bavarian National Cookbook*

162. Ben Katchor, *The Dairy Restaurant*

163. Pierre Louÿs, *The Young Girl's Handbook of Good Manners*

164. William S. Burroughs, 'Word', from *Interzone*

165. Edward F. Edinger, *Ego and Archetype*

166. Kenneth Hayes, *Milk and Melancholy*

167. Aristotle, *Historia Animalium*

168. Kenneth Hayes, *Milk and Melancholy*

169. Graham Robb, *Rimbaud*

170. George Melly, *Don't Tell Sybil*, (writing about his escapades with Edouard [ELT] Mesens)

171. Antonin Artaud, *Sound Panes*

172. Witold Gombrowicz, *Ferdydurke*

173. Wendy Doniger O'Flaherty, *Women, Androgynes, and Other Mythical Beasts*

174. Italo Calvino, 'The Distance of the Moon' in *Cosmicomics*

175. Nelson Hilton, 'Before the Milk of the Word: Nipple-Eyes', chapter two of *Lexis Complexes*

176. Wallace Stevens, *Men Made Out of Words*

177. Peter Blegvad, 'Alcohol'

178. *Webster's New International Dictionary*, second edition, 1934

179. Mina Loy, '#9', *Love Songs to Joannes*

180. Nelly Sachs, from 'Flight and Metamorphosis', trans. Joshua Weiner & Linda B. Parshall, in *Poetry*, April 2020

181. Maggie Nelson, *Bluets*

182. Carolyn Forché, 'On Earth', in the collection *Blue Hour*
183. Stephen King, *On Writing*
184. Isabella Gardner, *The Milkman*
185. David Antin, 'the sociology of art', from *talking at the boundaries*
186. Paul Metcalf, *I-57*
187. Richard Littler, footnote in *Discovering Scarfolk*
188. Franz Lidz, introduction to *LIFE*'s special issue 'Vampires: Their Undying Appeal'
189. Witold Gombrowicz, *Ferdydurke*
190. Hayden Herrera, *Frida: A Biography of Frida Kahlo*
191. Kenneth Hayes, *Milk and Melancholy*
192. Tom Robbins, *Even Cowgirls Get the Blues*
193. Lyric to 'Milk It' by Kurt Cobain on the album *In Utero*, by Nirvana
194. Gérard de Nerval, *Aurelia*
195. Marcel Duchamp, *The Green Box*
196. Gaston Bachelard, *Earth and Reveries of Will*, trans. Kenneth Haltman
197. Extract from book four of *Fragments from the Estate of a Young Physicist* by Johann Wilhelm Ritter (trans. Malcolm Green)
198. Georges Limbour, *The Panorama*, trans. Iain White
199. Anon, 'Schizophrenic Definitions', in *America: a Prophecy*, by Jerome Rothenberg & George Quasha
200. Marguerite Sechehaye, *Autobiography of a Schizophrenic Girl*
201. Roger Gilbert-Lecomte, 'Dance Night', in *Black Mirror*, trans. David Rattray
202. William Empson, 'Alice in Wonderland: The Child as Swain, on Alice's Adventures in Wonderland by Lewis Carroll', in *Alice's Adventures in Wonderland, Modern Critical Interpretations*, ed. Harold Bloom
203. Sarah Chalmers, *Daily Mail*, 14 April 2001
204. Robert Duncan, *Shadows*
205. Brian Aldiss
206. Roger Gilbert-Lecomte, 'Coronation and Massacre of Love', in *Black Mirror*, trans. David Rattray
207. George Oppen, *Sara in Her Father's Arms*
208. Søren Kierkegaard, *Fear and Trembling*
209. Stanley Elkin, *The Living End*
210. Clement of Alexandria
211. Job 21:24
212. Laura Shanley, 'Milkmen: Fathers Who Breastfeed', *unassistedchildbirth.com/inspiration/* (accessed 10 May 2023)
213. Iwan Bloch, *The Sexual Life of Our Time*
214. Aristotle, *Historia Animalium*
215. Philip Roth, *The Breast*
216. Uno Holmberg, *Mythology of All Races*, volume 4
217. Euripides, *The Bacchae*
218. Aristotle, *De Generatione Animalium*
219. Pierre Emmanuel, *Paris des Poètes*
220. Kate Connolly, *The Guardian*, 18 Oct. 2010
221. Clayton Eshleman, *An Anatomy of the Night*
222. D. H. Lawrence, *Sons and Lovers*
223. Vladislav Zadrobilek interviewed by Joseph Caezza, *levity.com/alchemy/caezza6.html* (accessed Aug. 2023)
224. Robert Graves, interview in *The Paris Review*, Summer 1969
225. Romain Gary, *The Life Before Us* ("Madame Rosa")
226. Gaston Bachelard, *On Poetic Imagination and Reverie*
227. Robin Blaser, 'and Bach lived that definition far better', from *The Holy Forest*
228. Paul Celan, *Death Fugue*
229. Jean Genet, *The Blacks*
230. Ralph Ellison, *Invisible Man*

231. W. E. B. Du Bois, *The Song of the Smoke*

232. Gaston Bachelard, *On Poetic Imagination and Reverie*, quoting from *L'homme ligoté* by J.-P. Sartre

233. Unica Zürn, *The Man of Jasmine*, trans. Malcolm Green

234. Ovid, 'Fasti', epigraph to *Milk*, poems by Dorothea Lasky

235. Lewis Carroll, *Through the Looking-Glass*

236. Steve Connor, article in either *The Guardian* or *The Independent*, title and date unknown

237. Wendy Doniger O'Flaherty, *Women, Androgynes, and Other Mythical Beasts*

238. Andrew Marantz, 'Birth of a Supremacist', *The New Yorker*, 16 Oct. 2017

239. Tim Lewis, 'How We Fell out of Love With Milk', *The Guardian*, 11 Nov. 2018

240. Elena Orde, 'How We Have Been Tricked into Thinking Milk Is Good for Us', *huffingtonpost.co.uk*

241. Laura Reiley, *The Washington Post*, 12 May 2023

242. Lautréamont, *Les Chants de Maldoror*, trans. Paul Knight

243. Fanny Howe, *My Father Was White but Not Quite*

244. Danez Smith, *Don't Call Us Dead*

245. Kenneth Hayes, *Milk and Melancholy*

246. Liam Shaw, 'Life Soup', a review of *Slime: A Natural History* by Susanne Wedlich, trans. Ayça Türkoğlu, *London Review of Books*, 21 April 2022

247. Terence McKenna, *True Hallucinations*

248. H. D., *Tribute to the Angels*

249. Aleister Crowley, *The Magical Record of the Beast 666*

250. H. G. Wells, *The Story of the Late Mr Elvesham*

251. Henri Frankfort, *Kingship and the Gods*, quoting Kurt Sethe, *Die altägyptischen Pyramidentexte*

252. Roger Gilbert-Lecomte, 'Notes for a Coming Attraction', in *Black Mirror*, trans. David Rattray

253. Witold Gombrowicz, *Ferdydurke*

254. Danez Smith, *Don't Call Us Dead*

255. Hans A. Halbey, 'Analyses and Research on Children's Reception of the Picture Book *In the Night Kitchen* by Maurice Sendak', address to the 15th Congress of the International Board on Books for Young People

256. Maurice Sendak, *In the Night Kitchen*

257. Jane Ellen Harrison, *Prolegomena to the Study of Greek Religion*

258. *The Job: Interviews with William S. Burroughs*, by William S. Burroughs, Daniel Odier

259. Sarah Manguso, *Ongoingness / 300 Arguments*

260. Samuel J. Crumbine & James A. Tobey, *The Most Nearly Perfect Food: The Story of Milk*

261. Unica Zürn, *The Man of Jasmine*, trans. Malcolm Green

262. *The American Heritage Dictionary of the English Language*, fifth edition

263. Wikipedia

264. Ben Katchor, quoting Franz Kafka, trans. Ian Johnston, in *The Dairy Restaurant*

265. Glen Baxter, 'Paying Attention', in *Almost Completely Baxter: New and Selected Blurtings*

266. Jane Bowles, *A Quarreling Pair*

267. Jane Ellen Harrison, *Themis*

268. Danez Smith, *Don't Call Us Dead*

269. A *pai-hua* ('plain speech') poem from Northern China, 'made new' by C. H. Kwock and G. G. Gach, in *Technicians of the Sacred*, ed. Jerome Rothenberg

270. Anon

271. Me

272. Frances Kennedy, 'Italian court says breasts are works of art', *The Independent on Sunday*, 3 Oct. 1999

273. H. L. Mencken, *The Lure of Beauty*

274. Nonnus, *The Dionysiaca*, quoted by Mervyn Levy in *The Moons of Paradise: Reflections on the Breast in Art*

275. Nelson Hilton, 'Before the Milk of the Word: Nipple-Eyes', chapter two of *Lexis Complexes*

276. Erasmus, *In Praise of Folly*

277. Hayden Herrera, *Frida: A Biography of Frida Kahlo*

278. Marguerite Sechehaye, *Autobiography of a Schizophrenic Girl*

279. Mark Ford, introduction to *The Alley of Fireflies and Other Stories*, by Raymond Roussel, trans. Mark Ford

280. Charles Arthur, 'Scientist links autism to bread and milk in diet', *The Guardian*, date unknown

281. Peter Conchie, 'Feline Frenzy' (an article about the artist Louis Wain, 'The Hogarth of Cat Life') in *The Independent*, 15 Aug. 1997

282. Louis Zukofsky, lines 147–152 of *Poem beginning 'The'*

283. Kenneth Hayes, in *Milk and Melancholy*

284. Ricky Jay, quoting John Bulwer, *Learned Pigs and Fireproof Women*

285. Robert Burton, *The Anatomy of Melancholy*

286. Susan Baur, *The Dinosaur Man: Tales of Madness and Enchantment from the Back Ward*

287. John Updike, review of Philip Roth's *The Anatomy Lesson*, in *The New Yorker*, 7 Nov. 1983

288. Stevie Smith, *The Wanderer*

289. Søren Kierkegaard, *Journal* (IV A 76, early May 1843)

290. Sudhir Kakar, *The Engulfing Mother in Indian Mythology: Masculinity and Conflicting Desires*

291. Marilyn Yalom, *A History of the Breast*

292. Robert Lindner, 'Songs My Mother Taught Me', from *The Fifty-Minute Hour*

293. Paul Metcalf, *I–57*

294. Nelson Hilton in *Lexis Complexes*, quoting Renato J. Almansi, 'The Face-Breast Equation', *Journal of the American Psychoanalytic Association* 8, no.1 (1960).

295. Herschell Gordon Lewis interviewed in *Incredibly Strange Film*, RE/search, no.10

296. Adrian Mitchell, *Peace is Milk*

297. Fiona MacCarthy, 'Skin Deep', a review of two books about cosmetic surgery in *The New York Review of Books*, 7 Oct. 1999

298. Anne Enright, 'My Milk', *London Review of Books*, 5 Oct. 2000

299. Nigel Lewis, *The Book of Babel*

300. Jack Kerouac, *Visions of Cody*

301. Aristotle, *De Generatione Animalium*

302. From 'a Hasidic text' quoted in *Encyclopedia of Esoteric Man*, by Benjamin Walker

303. Wikipedia, 'List of choking deaths'

304. Catherine Price, 'Breast Friends', *SLATE Review*, 6 July 2011

305. Review of Courtney Jung, *Lactivism: How Feminists and Fundamentalists, Hippies and Yuppies, and Physicians and Politicians Made Breastfeeding Big Business and Bad Policy* in *New York Times*, 14 Dec. 2015

306. Linda Gregerson, 'The Bad Physician', opening poem in the book *The Woman Who Died in Her Sleep*

307. Peter Blegvad, 'Breast Is Best', from 'Milk, Matter of Life and Death', in *The Phantom Museum*, ed. Hildi Hawkins and Danielle Olsen

308. Frans de Waal, *Bonobo: The Forgotten Ape*

309. Nancy Friday, *My Secret Garden, Women's Sexual Fantasies*

310. Alejandro Jodorowsky, *Where the Bird Sings Best*

311. Adrian Mitchell, *Peace Is Milk*

312. Terence McKenna, *True Hallucinations*

313. Malcolm de Chazal, *Sens-Plastique*, trans. Irving Weiss

314. Evelyn Waugh, Letter to Ann Fleming, 3/3/1964

315. M. Maier, 'Atalanta fugiens' (1618), in *Alchemy & Mysticism*, by Alexander Roob

316. Witold Gombrowicz, *Ferdydurke*

317. Josip Novakovich, 'In the Same Boat', *New Directions*, 55

318. Dylan Thomas, *When Once the Twilight Locks no Longer*

319. Palindrome quoted by Dmitri Borgmann in *Language on Vacation: an Olio of Orthographic Oddities*

320. Jeremy Laurance, 'Cream treatment for epilepsy', *The Independent*, 11 Nov. 1998

321. Aristotle, *Historia Animalium*

322. William Blake, *The Four Zoas*

323. *The New York Post*, date unknown (early '80s)

324. Blaise Cendrars, *Planus*

325. Charles Baudelaire, *Artificial Paradises*

326. Norman Douglas, *Siren Land*

327. Charles Olson, *Apollonius of Tyana*

328. Wikipedia entry re. 'Le Tentazioni del Dottor Antonio',

segment by Federico Fellini in the film *Boccaccio '70*

329. *New York Times*, date unknown

330. Zoe Beloff

331. Ian M. L. Hunter, *Memory*

332. Daniil Kharms, 'Stories about Himmelkumov', in *I Am a Phenomenon Quite Out of the Ordinary*, trans. Anthony Anemone & Peter Scotto

333. Henri Bergson, *Introduction to Metaphysics*, trans. T. E. Hulme

334. Kenneth Hayes, *Milk and Melancholy*

335. Dorothea Lasky, *Milk*

336. André Breton, *Sunflower*

337. David Coxhead, *Speed King*

338. Quoted in 'A midsummer night's sex comedy', Roger Ebert's review of Ingmar Bergman's *Smiles of a Summer Night*, rogerebert.com/reviews/great-movie-smiles-of-a-summer-night-1955 (accessed Aug. 2023)

339. Roland Barthes, 'Wine and Milk', from *Mythologies*

340. Luis Buñuel, *Cinema, Instrument of Poetry*

341. Gregory Corso, *Food*

342. David Antin, *Biography*, quoted by Kenneth Hayes in *Milk and Melancholy*